Anabaptist Witness

A Global Anabaptist and Mennonite Dialogue on Key Issues Facing the Church in Mission

VOLUME 9 / ISSU

Anabaptist Witness

A Global Anabaptist and Mennonite Dialogue on Key Issues Facing the Church in Mission

About

Anabaptist Witness is published twice a year (April and October) and is indexed in the ATLA Religion Database® (ATLA RDB®), http://www.atla.com. It is a publication of Anabaptist Mennonite Biblical Seminary, Mennonite Church Canada, and Mennonite Mission Network. The views expressed in *Anabaptist Witness* are those of the contributing writers and do not necessarily reflect the opinions of the partnering organizations.

Subscriptions, Additional Copies, and Change of Address

The annual subscription rate is $20 (US) plus shipping. Subscribers will receive an invoice to send with remittance to Anabaptist Mennonite Biblical Seminary. Single or additional copies of *Anabaptist Witness* are available for purchase through Amazon.com. Change of address or questions about purchasing the journal may be directed to the editor at the address below or by sending an email to subscriptions@anabaptistwitness.org.

Editorial Correspondence

The editor makes a public call for submissions for each issue of the journal, soliciting contributions that facilitate meaningful exchange among peoples from around the world, across professions, and from a variety of genres (sermons, photo-essays, interviews, biographies, poems, academic papers, etc.). All submissions to *Anabaptist Witness* undergo a double-blind peer review process. For full details of the current call for submissions, visit www.anabaptistwitness.org. Questions or comments about the journal's print or online content may be directed to the editor:

Jamie Pitts
JPitts@AMBS.edu

Copyright

ISSN 2374-2534 (print)
ISSN 2374-2542 (online)

Cover art: Matt Veith

Anabaptist Witness
Anabaptist Mennonite Biblical Seminary
3003 Benham Avenue
Elkhart, IN 46517 USA

www.anabaptistwitness.org

Anabaptist Witness

A global Anabaptist and Mennonite dialogue on key issues facing the church in mission

VOLUME 9 / ISSUE 1 / APRIL 2022

Mission & Formation

ARTICLES

REVIEWS

Editorial

How are Anabaptists formed for witness? Our vision for this issue of *Anabaptist Witness* is to call attention to such formation, broadly construed as a dynamic process where external and internal forces shape Anabaptists as persons and communities that, in turn, impact witness. As such, we cannot conceptualize Anabaptist witness without seeking an understanding of the formation that gives rise to this witness. This formation is situated, meaning that social, cultural, ethnic, racial, gender, socioeconomic, and other contextual aspects profoundly shape our lives and witness.

At the same time, how does engaging in witness form Anabaptists? The impact of witness is not one-directional; the act of narrating how faith has influenced one's life creates and hones frameworks of meaning for the witnessing person. Moreover, the recipient of witness—hopefully as a co-participant in the witnessing event—necessarily has an impact on the person who bears witness. Every context of witness, every intersection of experience and worldviews, has a formative effect on the witnesser because witnessing is done through deep dialogue—a space of mutual interaction and transformation. As guest editors, we build this issue of Anabaptist Witness on the cyclical premise that *Anabaptists are formed for witness* and that *witnessing forms Anabaptists.*

We believe that authentic Christian witness emerges when we faithfully practice the teachings of Jesus. As such, theological formation, ethics and discipleship, and witness and mission are deeply interconnected in many Anabaptist streams. Theological education aims to equip and form people to live out this calling of discipleship in society. Hence, theological education and formation undergird Christian witness.

Recent scholarship from theologians such as Willie James Jennings and Kwok Pui-lan has drawn our attention to the processes and products of formation. Analyses from Jennings, Kwok, and their colleagues in *After Whiteness: An Education in Belonging*, *Teaching Global Theologies: Power and Praxis*, and *Theology without Borders: An Introduction to Global Conversations* resound with a similar claim—theological education and formation in North America has been done predominantly through Western, Eurocentric, and individualistic lenses. Recipients of theological education in the church and academy alike are being formed into an image of the white, self-sufficient male. These voices sound an urgent challenge to diversify theological education and recognize the interconnectedness of formation, discipleship, and witness.

As Anabaptists whose vocation is located at the intersection of the church and the academy, we find formation into the hegemonic pattern of whiteness deeply problematic. For example, Mennonite churches in general privilege the "foundational" ethnicities—meaning Mennonites with Swiss, Dutch, Russian, and German backgrounds. As a result, their histories, faith stories, lived experiences, and theological perspectives are heavily centered. Those deemed "non-ethnic Mennonites" by the dominant cultural groups are often left minimal space to contribute to and influence the life and faith of the Mennonite churches in North America.

To counter this malformation and to enrich theological education and formation in our globalized and pluralist society, it is crucial to de-center the predominant lenses and to diversify and incorporate non-Western and traditionally marginalized voices, both in the academy and the church. These voices are calling for an evaluation of formation, and we hear them challenging Anabaptist witness in churches and schools in North America and beyond.

These voices also lead us as guest editors of this issue to ask self-critical questions: Whose theological insights do we typically utilize when we prepare a lesson, sermon, or academic paper? In response to this challenge, we have done curriculum audits and evaluated the sources for our sermons and scholarship in order to increase our reliance on sources that do not conform to whiteness. When we talk about Anabaptist/Mennonite identity and history, whose stories do we favor and whose experiences do we not count as Anabaptist? In seeking contributions to this issue, we have sought perspectives beyond dominant North American Mennonites of European descent, and we affirm as deeply Anabaptist those reflections from contributors whose identities are not white, male, non-disabled and located in the United States or Canada. Specifically, are white Anabaptists aware of how they are complicit—knowingly and unknowingly—with white supremacy, settler colonialism, and patriarchy when they engage in witness?

In light of this, we have included submissions in this issue that critique current patterns of Anabaptist/Mennonite education and formation and also offer constructive proposals rooted in authors' particular contexts and traditions. Some submissions reflect self-critically on the author's experience of formation and its impact on witness, while others explore the interconnectedness of formation, discipleship, and witness.

This issue seeks to promote a diversity of voices and to demonstrate the value of personal narrative, reflection that arises from congregational life, and academic scholarship. As such, a poem, personal reflections, and academic articles are interspersed to affirm these important theological contributions and facilitate creative imagination and learning that can arise from reading a rich diversity of perspectives and formats. Illustrative images also accompany some of the written pieces.

Sarah Werner's poem, "The Kin-dom of Heaven," foregrounds this issue. As someone with a visible disability, the author reflects where she has experienced belonging and acceptance and invites the readers to briefly dwell in an image of a summer camp. She depicts it as a place and space where humans are near to nature, people from diverse backgrounds can come together and enjoy each other's presence, and everyone feels belonging in the midst of their differences. Werner names this place and space as the kin-dom of heaven, because whiteness, ableism, or any other dominant-isms in society are de-centered and everyone is accepted just as they are. The poem, in a gentle way, encourages the readers what to unlearn and what to relearn as people of the kin-dom of heaven.

In "Icons of God in the World," Emily Ralph Servant examines traditional images of God as impassive and powerful and explains how these images have negatively influenced Christians' formation and witness. Moving beyond hegemonic images of God articulated and accepted as normative in white, male, Western perspectives, the author, based on the stories of Jesus, proposes a God who is relational and vulnerable. Through this shift of images, Servant argues that witnessing becomes dialogical and mutually transformative rather than unidirectional and seeking to convert the other. Christian formation thus occurs through encounters. In these encounters, Christians are aware that their understanding of God is limited, and they are open to learning more about God from others. The telos of this formation and witnessing, according to the author, is the unity in God and with God, where everyone experiences full belonging with their full selves, where differences are not erased but celebrated and viewed as gifts.

Robert Thiessen offers a personal reflection of his formation in mission at the intersection of indigenous Mexican culture and white missionary influence in "Formation for Witness: Anabaptist Lessons Learned Far from Home." Among the Metlatonoc Mixtecs, Thiessen experienced a profound formation in a new understanding of Anabaptism that he had not received in his Mennonite Brethren home community in Ontario, Canada. He recounts the impact of white non-Anabaptist missionaries as well as indigenous believers who taught him, in the context of their mutual participation in witness, core values of Anabaptism that he now holds dear.

Sarah Ann Bixler offers the image of the Möbius loop in "Mission as Distraction? A Critical Twist on Formation and Mission in Anabaptist Communities on the Möbius Loop" to illustrate the relationship between formation and witness. She conceives of the relationship as a perpetual inner-outer exchange, where the two co-create each other. Drawing from missional theologians within and beyond Anabaptism, Bixler points out a tendency she observes in Anabaptist thought and practice to either collapse formation and witness or to emphasize external witness as a distraction from unhealthy formation within the Anabaptist community. She explores a recent conflict in the LMC Anabaptist community in light of this latter concern, calling for renewed attention to both formation and witness in the life of the church in a way that honors each practice as distinct yet congruent.

In "Anabaptist Hermeneutical Formation and Witness in Meserete Kristos Church of Ethiopia," Endaweke Tsegaw explores how the formation of the Meserete Kristos Church (MKC) was influenced by North American Anabaptist missions. Examining early and recent Anabaptist biblical interpretation and theological emphases, Tsegaw identifies echoes of these commitments in the formation of MKC that emerged in the mid-twentieth century. He describes six formational Anabaptist practices in MKC: congregational hermeneutics, Christocentrism, nonviolent resistance, church and state relations, women as leaders in the church, and historical critical biblical interpretation. In conclusion, Tsegaw calls all Anabaptist Mennonite communities to likewise reflect on their formation and Anabaptist hermeneutical commitments that prepare them for witness.

Kimberly Penner analyzes malformative narratives about sexuality and their impact on Anabaptist witness and discipleship in "Formed as (Sexual) Peacemakers? Interrogating the Role of Sexuality in Relation to Institutional Culture for Formation for Witness and Discipleship at Postsecondary Theological Schools." By exploring religious narratives about sexuality and institutional culture in Anabaptist-Mennonite postsecondary institutions, she calls attention to the problems of discrimination and abuse currently inherent in the formation of students in peace and justice. Drawing on the insights of Willie James Jennings, Penner calls these institutions to resist malformation and be intentional about embodying cultures of peace and justice in relationship to sexual ethics, in order to form students with integrity for witness and discipleship.

Jennifer Davis Sensenig's article, "Formed for Witness by the Biblical Story," examines how some Mennonite pastors are utilizing the Narrative Lectionary, a ministry tool that schedules scripture readings based on the church year to assist congregational faith formation. The twenty-two pastors she interviewed reported being shaped by the biblical stories and, at the same time, deepening their understanding of the stories through connecting scripture texts with their own social contexts. The article indicates a few limitations of the material but strongly recommends it as a great tool to help congregations engage more with scripture and provide natural opportunities for them to be captivated by the sacred stories of the Bible. This approach to faith formation invites each reader and congregation to bring questions and struggles that emerge from their own unique contexts and experiences. And through this engagement with the sacred stories, the hope is that the people will discover good news to share with their communities, a message that deeply resonates with and transforms the lives of the people of those communities.

By highlighting the voices and experiences of these authors, we, as co-editors of this issue, hope to unsettle the predominant Anabaptist-Mennonite approaches of formation and witnessing so that more richly diverse approaches emerge within our academic institutions and churches. The book and film reviews that conclude the issue further this goal through reflections on the global church, race, and ecology. May these writings deepen and broaden our theological imagination and formation so that we can faithfully walk and witness as disciples of Jesus in an ever more pluralistic and diversified society and world.

Guest editors:

—Sarah Ann Bixler

Associate Dean of the Seminary and Assistant Professor of Formation and Practical Theology, Eastern Mennonite University, Harrisonburg, VA, USA

—Hyung Jin "Pablo" Kim Sun

Senior Leader for Anti-Racism and Intercultural Conciliation, Christian Reformed Church within Canada

The Kin-dom of Heaven

Sarah Werner

The kin-dom of heaven is a summer camp.
Mid-July in the flat piney woods of East Texas
the heat of a vibrant earth radiating on every surface in daylight,
with a soft cool breeze to soothe in the night,
which is loud with crickets and whippoorwills and barred owls.

The kin-dom of heaven is a summer camp.
We come with all our perceived imperfections—
rural accent, skin too dark, too light, blind, orphaned, widowed, gay,
five years old, eighty-five years old,
and
there is a place and task for
every
body:

> Counting the number of minutes from the first light of the pink dawn
> until the sun breaks over the trees onto the still water of the pond.
> Clearing the brush from the hiking trails.
> Tending the garden of spiders under the picnic tables.
> Sorting out the markers that still draw from the ones that are dried up.
> Watching the beauty of the day unfold
> content in the joy of being alive.

Sarah Werner is an educator, editor, and writer living in Columbus, Ohio. She is a worship leader and youth sponsor at Columbus Mennonite Church. She has Ehlers-Danlos Syndrome, an inherited connective tissue disorder that impairs her mobility. She enjoys hand-cycling, camping, and nature photography in her free time.

In the kin-dom of heaven that is summer camp
we gather to become more deeply who we are.
We come to learn that we are immeasurably stronger
and
more valuable
than we thought.
That we matter, belong, just because we are alive,
that our scars do not define us
but add beauty to the sharp edge of our lives.

I want the kin-dom of heaven to be this place,
because I need somewhere to belong
as my whole self,
to be seen for all of who I am,
not what I lack or
what I've lost.

I want to be more than my fragile, painful, too-tense body,
more than my wheelchair,
than my bulky muscle arms, than my skinny legs,
more than the words on my tongue and in my mind,
more than the thoughts I pour onto the page, and
my education and
my family and
my upbringing.

I want to feel with keenness that I am strong for what I do have,
which is my soul-being.
I want to know that there is a place to belong
even if I am no longer sharp-witted,
even if I can no longer move on my own,
even if I don't "contribute" to society,
that my just being alive is still a blessing for the world,

that I am not
one person
alone
but part of a web of family, given and chosen.

Icons of God in the World

Mission as Formation

Emily Ralph Servant

In Christian tradition, the word "formation" has been associated with the transformation of a Jesus-follower into the image of Christ, God in the flesh.[1] The Anabaptist tradition contains rich resources to shape a missional posture around our identity as God's image-bearers. For many early Anabaptists, the call to follow Jesus meant a total transformation, what Menno Simons called "The New Birth."[2] Through the life, death, and resurrection of Jesus and the presence of the Spirit, these radical disciples believed that the image of God within each person was reawakened, allowing them to make a decision to follow God and participate in God's life.[3] This reawakening, or "divinization," was manifested as a visible new way of life that transformed the follower of Jesus into God's image and brought them into community with God.[4] Significantly, this understanding of the "reawakening" of the image of God in each person assumes that each person already has the image of God present within them—God's image within has just been lost, tarnished, or twisted. All of humanity has been created in God's image; as one grows in their unity with God, the image of God within becomes more visible, more recognizable, more authentic.

If the goal of formation is to be transformed into the image of Jesus, the icon[5] of God, then formation is shaped by our image of God. Additionally, the

---

Emily Ralph Servant is a writer, theologian, and Leadership Minister for Mosaic Mennonite Conference. She lives with her family in Baltimore City, where she teaches—and mostly learns—about God, mission, and being transformed by the creative Spirit.

1 2 Cor 3:18.

2 Menno Simons, "A Fundamental Doctrine from the Word of the Lord, of the New Birth," in *The Complete Works of Menno Simons*, Vol I, trans. John Funk (Elkhart, IN: John F. Funk & Brother, 1871): 167–76.

3 Frances F. Hiebert, "The Atonement in Anabaptist Theology," *Direction* 30, no. 2 (2001): 122–38.

4 Hiebert, 128.

5 Throughout this article, I will interchange the traditional phrase "image of God" with the phrase "icon of God." In English, the word "icon" has additional connotations as "a representation (as in a mural, a mosaic, or a painting . . .) . . . of a sacred individual"

image of God that we bear influences our witness as we live as icons of God in the world. What image of God does the world see when they look at us? In this article, I suggest that traditional images of God as impassive and powerful (omniscient, omnipotent, and omnibenevolent) have often been reflected in the missionary enterprise. In response, I propose an expansion of our concept of God in mission by exploring stories of Jesus through a lens of vulnerability and mutuality. I suggest that these images of Jesus can help to form us into communities that acknowledge the presence of God in the Other and consent to our own conversion as we seek to not only *be* but also *see* icons of God in the world. I then offer three spiritual practices that can position us to be transformed into communities willing to risk vulnerable relationships with our neighbors as a reflection of the God whose image we bear.

A note about my social location: As a white feminist Anabaptist theologian and pastor in the Mennonite tradition, from the stream of "Old Mennonites" that became part of Mennonite Church USA,[6] I write from a middle-class, rapidly changing, and increasingly diverse community of churches based on the East Coast of the United States.[7] While I hope that the ideas contained in this article will be helpful to folks beyond my context, I am primarily addressing long-time church members in traditional, predominantly white Mennonite congregations.

A Tarnished Image

The images we have of God, the structures of church life, and our understandings of the how and why of mission were all developed within the context of church leaders for their time and place. While this in itself was not necessarily problematic, suggests Cherokee pastor and mission worker Randy Woodley, the difficulty came when these church leaders "normalized and universalized their context to fit the whole world."[8] While causation is beyond the scope of

---

(*Merriam-Webster.com Dictionary*, s.v. "icon," accessed March 8, 2022, https://www.merriam-webster.com/dictionary/icon). Thus, an "icon" is something that can be tangibly experienced.

6 "Old Mennonites" is a popular term for the "Mennonite Church" denomination, which merged with the General Conference Mennonite Church to form Mennonite Church USA in 2002. See Harold S. Bender and Beulah Stauffer Hostetler, "Mennonite Church (MC)," Global Anabaptist Mennonite Encyclopedia Online (January 2013), accessed March 8, 2022, https://gameo.org/index.php?title=Mennonite_Church_(MC)&oldid=173394.

7 Mosaic Mennonite Conference: http://mosaicmennonites.org. I am grateful to my colleagues Marta Castillo and Noel Santiago for their conversation around this article.

8 Randy S. Woodley, "Mission and the Cultural Other: In Search of the Pre-colonial Jesus," *Missiology: An International Review* 43, no. 4 (2015): 467.

this article, we will explore one such contextualization and the harm caused as the church engaged in a model of mission that reflects this incomplete, and sometimes tarnished, image of God.

In the early church, theologians interpreted the oral and written stories about the life of Jesus and the teachings of the apostolic letters through their own cultural lenses as they sought to make sense of and defend the faith—sometimes to a hostile society and sometimes against perceived heresies within the church.[9] This contextualization within the framework of a Hellenistic worldview eventually led to what became traditional images of God as omnipotent, omniscient, and omnibenevolent[10] (and therefore immutable). The concept of God as the perfection of virtue and form (of which humans are only imperfect reflections) was developed by Greek philosophers Plato and Aristotle and found willing reception among some of the church's early theologians.[11] It was not a stretch, therefore, for some early church leaders to interpret the message of Jesus through the structures of Roman life built on Greek philosophy and political systems. Woodley observes how the message of freedom that Jesus taught and lived was quickly coopted into hierarchical models of governance and arguments about divine subordination and apostolic succession.[12] The servanthood of Jesus was replaced by an embrace of power and justified by a theology of God's sovereignty, which is still a foundational theme in missional theology today.[13]

Later theologians further developed concepts of Greek metaphysics as part of their Christian conceptions of God's essence and character.[14] In the conflation of church and state that developed, mission was driven by Jesus's words in Luke 14:23: "Compel them to come in."[15] This directive, most often expressed

---

9 See John Sanders, *The God Who Risks: A Theology of Divine Providence* (Downers Grove, IL: IVP Academic, 2009), 145, on the impact of the Arian debate on formulations of divine impassibility, for example.

10 In raising questions about our image of God as omnibenevolent, I am challenging not the concept of God's goodness but our interpretation of the nature of goodness. Who gets to decide what counts as "good," and can people from outside a culture have enough knowledge (omniscience) to define goodness or ethics on behalf of those inside a given culture? Therefore, it is not necessarily omnibenevolence in itself that can be problematic but linking it with omniscience and omnipotence.

11 Sanders, *God Who Risks*, 141–42.

12 Woodley, "Mission and the Cultural Other," 458.

13 Gene L. Green, "The Death of Mission: Rethinking the Great Commission," *Journal of the North American Institute for Indigenous Theological Studies* 12 (2014): 95.

14 Sanders, *God Who Risks*, 149–51.

15 David J. Bosch, *Transforming Mission: Paradigm Shifts in Theology of Mission* (Maryknoll, NY: Orbis, 1991), 236.

through forced conversions of Jews and pagans, expanded at times during the Protestant Reformation to include the conversions of people who defected to new Christian churches. This mandate, alongside views of God's sovereignty, power, and benevolence, accompanied the Catholic Church in overseas campaigns for land, resources, and converts.[16]

The new Protestant churches did not improve much upon the Catholic models of mission. They continued the interrelationship between church and state that provided both with additional power and sovereignty.[17] That authority reflected the absolute sovereignty of God, who took the initiative in going to humanity for their salvation. As the true representatives of God on earth, church leaders "were convinced that they had both the ability and the will to remake the world in their own image."[18]

The Enlightenment only served to further develop the Western church's sense of responsibility for and superiority over the rest of the world. There was a growing confidence in the "doctrine of progress," along with a belief that Western Christians could and should make the world right, utilizing colonial systems to do so: just as an all-benevolent, all-knowing, and all-powerful God sent a representative to save the world in Jesus, so the benevolent, wise, and powerful church (linked to the benevolent, wise, and powerful state) sent representatives to save the world. The scientific method of observation, experimentation, and analysis led to a tendency to treat people of other cultures as objects to be studied and acted upon rather than equal subjects.[19] Salvation, for the "heathens" of the world, included being "civilized" into the Western (superior) image.[20]

While the church has increasingly critiqued and rejected colonial models of mission over the past century, vestiges of those models have continued to shape how the church of the West—Mennonites included—engages in mission. Although Anabaptist streams like the Mennonites advocated against the connection between church and state, they still benefitted from the structures that those unholy alliances created, settling on land taken from indigenous peoples in the United States and participating in commerce supported by colonial networks.[21] The earliest Mennonite settlers in the United States, surrounded as they were by like-minded immigrants who did not need to be converted, rarely

16 Bosch, 226–30.

17 Bosch, 240.

18 Bosch, 265.

19 Bosch, 342–44.

20 Michael Bamwesigye Badriaki, *When Helping Works: Alleviating Fear and Pain in Global Missions* (Eugene, OR: Wipf & Stock, 2017), 11.

21 For more on the link between the Doctrine of Discovery and mission, see Green, "The Death of Mission."

participated in mission.[22] Over the following centuries, as more diverse immigrants settled around them, the Mennonite communities often withdrew into themselves as a protectionary reaction to the threat of identity-loss.[23]

At the turn of the twentieth century, however, some Mennonites in the United States observed the missionary movement, and, fed by the fervor of American revivalism, began to call for the establishment of missionary agencies for both international and domestic mission, modeled after the agencies they witnessed in other denominations.[24] Even as Mennonite participation in mission grew in the early twentieth century, it tended to happen in distant locations, both across the ocean and in urban centers or rural mission outposts. Benevolent, wise, and powerful (resource-rich) Mennonites brought the good news to the cultural "Other."

As a result, new converts were often very different from the missionaries who served them.[25] One church leader observed that many congregations preferred mission work at a distance because "they feared that new Christians from non-Mennonite backgrounds might bring a 'different cultural and religious climate' into the Church."[26] These new believers were kept separate from existing Mennonite churches for many decades;[27] church leaders struggled to discern to what extent converts must conform to Mennonite distinctives in faith and practice.[28] As some Mennonites became more involved in the ecumenical church movement, they began to shift their witness to the broader church and government.[29] Former mission worker Alan Kreider acknowledged a tendency of Mennonites in recent decades to focus evangelism on winning other Christians to the Mennonite values of peace and justice,[30] remaking them in our own image.

---

22 C. J. Dyck, *An Introduction to Mennonite History: A Popular History of the Anabaptists and the Mennonites* (Scottdale, PA: Herald, 1993), 197, 214.

23 Dyck, 198.

24 Theron F. Schlabach, *Gospel versus Gospel: Mission and the Mennonite Church, 1863–1944* (Scottdale, PA: Herald, 1980), 83.

25 John Ruth, *Maintaining the Right Fellowship* (Scottdale, PA: Herald, 1984), 417, 486. Schlabach describes how segregation at first led to benevolence for local people of color but not integration (*Gospel*, 76–78). See also my account of the Norristown, PA, mission in Emily Ralph, "God's Dream on Earth: New Narratives for the Intercultural Church" (MA thesis, Eastern Mennonite Seminary, Harrisonburg, VA, 2013), 77–78.

26 J. D. Graber, as quoted by Schlabach, *Gospel*, 238.

27 Schlabach, *Gospel*, 76–78.

28 Schlabach, 167–94.

29 Ervin R. Stutzman, *From Nonresistance to Justice: The Transformation of Mennonite Church Peace Rhetoric, 1908–2008* (Scottdale, PA: Herald, 2011), 142.

30 Alan Kreider, "Tongue Screws and Testimony," ed. James R. Krabill, *MissioDei* 16 (Elkhart, IN: Mennonite Mission Network, 2008).

Across the ideological and theological spectrum—from traditional evangelism to humanitarian or justice work—the image of the benevolent, knowledgeable, and powerful God still lurks behind the missionary enterprise. Ugandan development leader Michael Bamwesigye Badriaki suggests that the impact of Social Darwinism can still be felt in global mission programs through the promotion of "the survival of the fittest and superior culture over the 'cultural other.'"[31] As a result, "missionary fundraising and Christian humanitarianism have historically been set up to communicate fear through the portrayal of the missionized as stereotypically inferior. The system is set up to portray the people that God has called you to serve as less than you."[32] Imagery of God as "Ruler, Lord, Master, and Warrior" conveyed that Christianity was a religion for the elite, the upper-class, and those who wielded power.[33]

One lasting legacy of the Enlightenment is the expectation that sowing seeds will produce fruit: if someone who is knowledgeable plans an intervention, it will work (omniscience and omnipotence).[34] Ethicist Sharon Welch suggests that many middle-class Christians in the West organize their justice and mercy work around an ethic of control,[35] believing that it is their job to make sure everything turns out right.[36] Welch directly links this ethic of control to theology that describes God as omnipotent. She argues that absolute power, even attributed to God, "assumes that the ability to act regardless of the response of others is a good rather than a sign of alienation from others."[37] An ethic of control can simply be thinly veiled paternalism (omniscience and omnibenevolence).

Paternalism also takes the form of the "trajectory of progress," the (sometimes unspoken) belief that "look[s] at the past as moving from less civilized to more civilized."[38] Woodley describes how, in the name of "civilization," missionaries have often created "systemic changes among colonized peoples that replaced their traditional values without regarding whether or not their traditional values align with Christ and his teachings"[39] (omniscience). This includes the assumption that development work based on best practices will lead to a

---

31 Badriaki, *When Helping Works*, 21.

32 Badriaki, 24.

33 Beverly Mitchell et al, "Mission from the Margins," *International Review of Mission* 101, no. 1 (2012): 157.

34 Bosch, *Transforming Mission*, 342.

35 Sharon D. Welch, *A Feminist Ethic of Risk* (Minneapolis: Fortress, 1990), 113.

36 Welch, 15.

37 Welch, 111.

38 Woodley, *Mission*, 462.

39 Woodley, 463.

better society (omnibenevolence).[40] Even a more recent desire to rescue global Christians from the effects of what we now consider to be "bad theology" introduced by previous Western missionaries has continued this narrative of progress: "'Soft' colonization is still colonization."[41]

In his critique of the popular book *When Helping Hurts*,[42] Badriaki wonders why Western definitions of "hurt" and success (omnibenevolence) are used to evaluate the effectiveness of missionary engagement. He suggests that the Western mission or development worker's tendency to refuse direct giving in the name of asset-based development[43] actually reflects a colonial (omniscient) mindset, in which the outsider knows what is best for the locals. This ends up portraying the recipients of mission "as incompetent, uncaring, 'always needy,' and inherently lacking in intellect."[44] The resulting stereotype suggests that the recipients of mission are not problem solvers but are themselves the problem.[45]

Much mission (including evangelism, justice, mercy, and development work) is designed around a model that sends out Western representatives with the truth, solution, or salvation (omniscience). Womanist theologian and anthropologist Linda Thomas connects this outward missionary movement to the Great Commission, which has focused attention on the command to "go and teach."[46] In joining forces with colonialism, the Great Commission has been interpreted as a command for Christians to "go over the world telling people about their God and teaching Western ways."[47] Christian mission has been a movement designed to spread a timeless, previously defined knowledge—described as the good news—which means that the missionary's posture is always that of "telling, curing, [and] saving" (omniscience and omnipotence).[48] This missionary posture reflects a dominant image of God as all-knowing, powerful, good, and unchanging—whether or not its practitioners acknowledge or endorse such a view.

---

40 Consider the implications of the term "developing world."

41 Green, "Death of Mission," 90.

42 Steve Corbett and Brian Fikkert, *When Helping Hurts: How to Alleviate Poverty without Hurting the Poor—and Yourself* (Chicago: Moody, 2014).

43 Badriaki's critique arises out of Corbett and Fikkert's assertion in *When Helping Hurts* that an outsider harms a community by meeting a need directly instead of empowering the community to find its own solution (a principle of asset-based community development) (Corbett and Fikkert, 25; Badriaki, *When Helping Works*, 20).

44 Badriaki, *When Helping Works*, 20.

45 Randy Woodley, forward to Badriaki, *When Helping Works*, viii.

46 Linda E. Thomas, "Anthropology, Mission, and the African Woman," in *Mission and Culture*, ed. Stephen B. Bevans (Maryknoll, NY: Orbis, 2012), 120.

47 Thomas, 120.

48 Thomas, 122.

Liberating the Image of Jesus

The concept of mission as a person of power lowering themselves to enter the world of someone inferior to elevate that inferior person to a higher level of living points to the very first agent of the *missio Dei*, the missionary God.[49] When seen through this lens, Jesus could be understood as the image of the impassive, benevolent, powerful, and all-knowing God—the Messiah come to establish a new kingdom based on a higher principle in the journey toward perfection. This image is of Jesus as the quintessential Colonizer. Members of the World Council of Churches' Just and Inclusive Communities program suggest that Jesus has become

> the captive saviour of the captive church. Jesus must first regain his own freedom, if he is to bestow it on others. This task cannot be accomplished either by the reactionary fundamentalist theology or reformative liberal theology of the privileged. Only the theology and practice of the despised, the marginalized, and the disinherited can liberate mission and the captive church.[50]

As members of a "Jesus-centered" tradition,[51] Anabaptists are well positioned to dig deeper into the stories of Jesus in the Gospels to discover how expanded images of God might change our practice of mission and formation. Missional practitioners Alan Hirsch and Michael Frost suggest that while it is true "that Jesus is like God," the greater truth is that God is like Jesus. For Hirsch and Frost, this means that the stories of Jesus in the Gospels should redefine our concepts of God while also modeling for us what it means to be truly human.[52]

No one can simply point to the Gospel accounts of the life of Jesus and expect a straightforward reading, however, even as, traditionally, some Anabaptist theologians have claimed a "simple reading" is possible.[53] As humans, we cannot avoid the influence of our social locations, life experiences, and theological or religious traditions on our biblical interpretation.[54] After generations of imitating a harmful image of God in the world, we are called to conversion. The historic

---

49 Bosch, *Transforming Mission*, 389–90.

50 Mitchell et al, "Mission from the Margins," 158.

51 As articulated in the popular credo from Palmer Becker, "Jesus is the center of our faith." See *Anabaptist Essentials: Ten Signs of a Unique Christian Faith* (Harrisonburg, VA: Herald, 2017).

52 Michael Frost and Alan Hirsch, *ReJesus: A Wild Messiah for a Missional Church* (Peabody, MA: Hendrickson, 2009), 12–13.

53 Walter Klaassen, *Anabaptism: Neither Catholic nor Protestant* (Kitchener, ON: Pandora, 2001), 40–51.

54 Miguel A. De La Torre, *Reading the Bible from the Margins* (Maryknoll, NY: Orbis, 2013), 1–3.

models of mission discussed above have been harmful to not only the recipients of them but also to those of us who have been formed as practitioners of them. A genuine image of God lies within us, but that image has been tarnished by a false image of God, an idol. Until we can strip away the remnants of those thought patterns, practices, and expectations, we will not be able to bring our authentic selves to others as the gift that God intended.

One challenge in rediscovering the image of God beneath the idol is that we often are not aware of the ways that our cultures and contexts have shaped our perceptions. Frequently, it is not until we encounter someone who sees the world differently that we grow conscious of our own lenses and interpretations.[55] Therefore it is difficult for us to change our images of God on our own; we are transformed through encounters—and even more so, through relationships—with God and with others. In this way, not only is formation missional but mission is formational.

To be transformed through encounters with others, however, we must be open to recognizing an image of God in them that may look unfamiliar. At the time the Creation story was written, as writer and activist Lisa Sharon Harper points out, a common cultural understanding considered only a select portion of the population to reflect the image of God. In contrast, by claiming that all humans bear God's "image," the biblical writers were introducing the radical concept that God could be found in everyone and that, as "image-bearers," each person had the right to exercise dominion—that is, to contribute to the common good of the world. Harper suggests that bearing God's image identifies each person as belonging to God; when we ignore that image in others or when we destroy that image by preventing others from exercising dominion, we are declaring war on God.[56]

God showed us a different way. When God "moved into the neighborhood,"[57] God chose to give up the privileges of existing outside of the mess of the world and became a human, an immigrant, right in the thick of it.[58] Jesus was the image of the invisible God,[59] the "word" or expression of God,[60] an "icon" of God to show us what God is like.[61] Yet Jesus did not model a faraway

55 See Emily Ralph Servant, *Experiments in Love: An Anabaptist Theology of Risk-Taking in Mission* (Eugene, OR: Pickwick, 2021), 30.

56 Lisa Sharon Harper, "#Lynchburg Revival Sermon," Red Letter Christians, September 20, 2018, accessed March 8, 2022. Video, 29:18. https://youtu.be/3YWJzWX-DWcY.

57 John 1:14, MSG.

58 Phil 2:5–11.

59 Col 1:15–20.

60 John 1:1.

61 John 14:6–10.

God; he modeled what humanity made in the image of God, in relationship with God, looks like. This God "is best understood, not in the ancient Greek philosophical notions of divinity as a master of perfection, who is aloof in divine omniscience, omnipotence, and impassibility [but] in the freedom of vulnerability."[62]

In modeling how to live as a vibrant icon of God in the world, Jesus showed this vulnerability by depending on his family and community to survive childhood. He relied on others around him to teach him the culture and social expectations of his community.[63] As an artisan's son, and described as a builder himself,[64] he needed his father to teach him a trade. He learned the language of his community, and he studied the Scriptures in religious spaces.[65] He depended on his community to teach him how to be human as a first-century Jewish man.

Yet Jesus also modeled a dependency beyond that of his community. Jewish feminist theologian Judith Plaskow has argued that Jesus did not introduce new teachings about women, justice, or the authority of Rome; there were other rabbis teaching similar concepts.[66] At the same time, still other rabbis were claiming to represent the voice of God while advocating for religious practices that conflicted with the teachings of Jesus. In the midst of the clamor of voices, Jesus modeled what it looks like to recognize the voice of God in the world around us. Jesus watched for what the Spirit of God was doing and then moved to align himself with it.

Jesus demonstrates this awareness and alignment in an encounter he had with an immigrant who asked for help.[67] At first, Jesus told her that he was limiting his healing ministry to his own people. When the woman challenged him to expand his focus, however, Jesus recognized the image of God in her face and the voice of God in her words. He realized that God was already working and chose to consent to the Spirit's energy moving through him. He healed the

---

62 Mitchell et al, "Mission from the Margins," 159.

63 Note Jesus's ability to integrate culturally relevant imagery in his parables. In Luke 15, for instance, Jesus tells stories that integrate social expectations around father-son relationships and inheritance, knowledge of agricultural practices, and even an understanding of how much a laborer makes in a day of work.

64 Matt 13:55 and Mark 6:3.

65 Luke 2:46.

66 Judith Plaskow, "Feminist Anti-Judaism and the Christian God," in *The Strength of Her Witness: Jesus Christ in the Global Voices of Women*, ed. Elizabeth A. Johnson (Maryknoll, NY: Orbis, 2016), 92–97.

67 Mark 7:24–30.

woman's daughter, affirmed her faith, and continued in a ministry that more clearly reflected the image of God in him.[68]

Perhaps Jesus was thinking about this woman when he told the parable of the widow bothering a judge until the judge relented.[69] Perhaps Jesus was thinking about the woman who washed his feet as an act of love[70] when he washed the feet of his disciples.[71] Perhaps Jesus was thinking of his own mother's care when he described God as a mother hen wanting to hide her chicks under her wings.[72] In using what Womanist Bible scholar Wil Gafney describes as our "sanctified imagination,"[73] we can see ways that Jesus's ministry may have been shaped by those he encountered.

Jesus modeled for us how to be transformed by the Other. Regardless of what old images of an immutable God have depicted, the life of Jesus implies that change is not a sin. Jesus's encounter with the immigrant woman suggests that a sin might actually occur if we were to recognize the Spirit in the Other and refuse to change in response. Perhaps this is what Jesus meant by an "unforgiveable sin" against God's Spirit[74]—attributing the work of the Spirit to evil forces.[75] If we watch for her, we can recognize the Spirit by her fruit.[76]

Jesus not only learned from others but also received their care and nurture. A group of women provided for Jesus and his disciples from their own financial resources;[77] other people—including "tax collectors and sinners"—fed Jesus and his disciples at their own tables;[78] some of the women of Jesus's community were present with him in his final moments on the cross;[79] another disciple provided

---

68 See Wil Gafney, "The Woman Who Changed Jesus," The Rev. Wil Gafney, Ph.D./ Womanists Wading in the Word, August 20, 2017, accessed March 8, 2022, https://www.wilgafney.com/2017/08/20/the-woman-who-changed-jesus/.

69 Luke 18:1–8.

70 John 12:1–3.

71 John 13:2–15.

72 Matt 23:37.

73 Wilda Gafney, *Womanist Midrash: A Reintroduction to the Women of the Torah and the Throne* (Louisville, KY: Westminster John Knox, 2017), 3.

74 Matt 12:22–37.

75 Gerald F. Hawthorne, *The Presence and the Power* (Dallas: Word, 2003), 172.

76 Matt 12:33.

77 Luke 8:1–3.

78 Luke 10:38–42. See Amos Yong, *Hospitality and the Other: Pentecost, Christian Practices, and the Neighbor* (Maryknoll, NY: Orbis, 2003), 101–3 for Jesus as both host and guest.

79 Matt 27:55–61; Mark 15:40, 47; Luke 23:49–55; and John 19:25.

a final resting place.[80] Jesus seemed to be deeply invested in his friendships with Martha, Mary, and Lazarus;[81] in moments of great stress, he sought solace in the company of his closest friends.[82] Jesus accepted the mutuality of these give-and-take relationships.

When Jesus sends out his disciples to engage in the work of mission in Luke 9, his instructions reflect a similar posture of mutuality and vulnerability. Yes, the disciples are given authority to perform acts of liberation and to share the good news, but they are also expected to do their work with a certain humility, as a guest. Thomas describes this mission as "radical" and "Jesus-like":

> [The disciples] go out as beggars; they have nothing to give. . . .
>
> The disciples do not bring God to others; no introduction is necessary. God's image greets them at the door; the Word comes to them when a stranger outside the gate says, "I have some extra bread if you're hungry." The disciples' work has nothing to do with changing others and everything to do with changing themselves. We do not create the kin-dom; we receive it when we are invited in just as we are, accepted by the *imago Dei* of a stranger who offers to wash our dirty feet.[83]

Icons of God in the World

These glimpses into the life of Jesus present a more nuanced image of God than the all-powerful, all-knowing, all-benevolent God of traditional mission. If this is the image of God that is forming us, like Jesus we relate to others in our communities and our world in fresh ways. We realize that we not only present the image of God *to* the world (mission) but also find the image of God *in* the world and are changed as a result (formation). Woodley describes the integration of formation and mission as a realization that "God expects two conversions out of every missional encounter: (1) our conversion to the truths in their culture, and (2) their conversion to the truth we bring to the encounter." He argues that it is first the responsibility of the church to adapt to others, and then, after much time, if "they invite us to share the gospel they have noticed us living out," we can share our (carefully contextualized) good news.[84]

Significantly, the practices of mission and formation are not solitary acts. Asian feminist theologian Kwok Pui-lan describes the "radical relationality" of

80 Mark 15:42–47.

81 Luke 10:38–42; John 11:1–44, 12:1–11.

82 Matt 17:1–2, 26:36–46.

83 Thomas, "Anthropology, Mission, and the African Woman," 130.

84 Woodley, "Mission and the Cultural Other," 466.

human existence: "A person does not exist in isolation, but in the web of relationship in which she finds herself."[85] The church, together, is an icon of God in the world: the body of Jesus, made of many parts—a mosaic.[86] The church is not *modeled after* the Trinitarian community of God, suggests Catholic feminist theologian Catherine Mowry LaCugna, but has been invited to *participate in* the life of the Trinity, welcomed into (re)union with God.[87] God's "dynamic movement" is "outward, a personal self-sharing by which God is forever bending toward God's 'other,'"[88] inviting humanity into a loving relationship. At its best, the church in union with God is a reflection of God's very self.

As an icon made of many pieces, however, the church will not accurately reflect the image of God if some of its parts are missing. The church will continue to be an incomplete icon until all of humanity has been welcomed into God's community, sharing God's life.[89] Therefore mission is inseparable from formation, transforming the church into a clearer and clearer image of God as "they" become "us," and we all join God's dynamic movement of bending toward others.

The Other does not become one of "us" by being replicated into our image, however; in that case, we would be forming them into an idol. Rather, the Other becomes one of "us" when we create space for them to belong as fully themselves and when we change our church structures and systems in response to what their presence among us brings to light, creating a new "us." This is a process in which we "reconcile the disparate parts, for people to remember their stories and who they are. . . . It is about being restored to one's rightful place in the community, about bringing together all the different pieces of the puzzle in order to complete the picture."[90] As we recognize "our common gift of the image of God," we together strive to love our neighbor as ourselves.[91]

Reawakening (to) the Image of God

In mission, we encounter God in the Other, and when we consent to being changed by those encounters, we reflect the image of God more fully, together. In this way, formation and mission are interconnected as essential to the life

---

85 Kwok Pui-lan, *Introducing Asian Feminist Theology* (Sheffield, England: Sheffield Academic, 2000), 78.

86 1 Cor 12:12–27.

87 Catherine Mowry LaCugna, *God for Us: The Trinity and Christian Life* (San Francisco: HarperSanFrancisco, 1991), 332.

88 LaCugna, 222.

89 Ralph Servant, *Experiments in Love*, 163–34.

90 Mitchell et al, "Mission from the Margins," 162.

91 Mitchell et al, 163.

of the church. To reawaken the image of the vulnerable God within us, we are invited to participate in spiritual practices that position us for transformation. At the intersection of these encounters with God, ourselves, and others, we may experience rebirth.

Practice One: Exploring New Images of God

The Bible is full of stories that have been used for harm, but it also contains stories of God that can challenge our old ways of thinking and acting. We can intentionally look to re-narrate[92] stories of God in the Bible through the lens of Jesus and through the experience of the Other. This involves emphasizing different narratives, finding new meaning in familiar stories, and exploring how our worldviews shape our biblical interpretations. This practice includes reading, listening, and watching theological reflections by those who are an "other" to us because of their ethnicity, socioeconomic status, religious background, gender identity, politics, or life experience. We can also benefit from studying the Bible with people who are still beginning their journey with Jesus, have not yet committed themselves to Christian faith, or who are skeptical of the Bible's value in everyday life.

As we contemplate the icons of God revealed in these interactions, we encounter the living God and are transformed in the process. "By emptying ourselves of concepts and images of God, or of expectations about what God is or should be or should be doing," suggests LaCugna, "we become free to know and love the real living God instead of the God of our projections."[93]

Practice Two: Connecting with Our Own Cultural Giftedness

Whether we identify as "white" or have a deeper connection to an ethnic identity, "whitewashing" has tarnished the image of God in many of us.[94] At the same time, "whiteness" has blinded us to the intersections of experience and cultures

---

92 The concept of "re-narrating" stories from the Bible comes from the field of narrative therapy, which suggests that "in any life there are always more events that don't get 'storied' than there are ones that do"; therefore, "when life narratives carry hurtful meanings or seem to offer only unpleasant choices, they can be changed by highlighting different, previously un-storied events or by taking new meaning from already-storied events, thereby constructing new narratives." Jill Freedman and Gene Combs, *Narrative Therapy* (New York: W. W. Norton: 1996), 32–33. See also Ralph Servant, *Experiments in Love*, 31–36.

93 Catherine Mowry LaCugna, "The Trinitarian Mystery of God," in *Systematic Theology: Roman Catholic Perspectives*, ed. Catherine Mowry LaCugna (Minneapolis: Fortress, 1991), 157.

94 Harper, "#Lynchburg Revival Sermon." Harper describes how the legal rights associated with a "white" identity caused immigrants to the United States throughout

that make each person unique.[95] A spiritual practice of reconnecting with our own cultural giftedness requires the painful work of stripping away the layers of racism, sexism, colonialism, capitalism, classism, and other "isms" that have infiltrated our ways of acting and interacting in the world. To help with this process, we can learn about cultural difference[96] and challenge ourselves to make our implicit assumptions explicit.[97] We can listen to the experiences of those different from ourselves, explore family traditions and stories, and reflect on the elements that combine to shape our identities and worldviews. This practice can be expanded to include communal exploration as congregations discover the diversity within and together recognize and change practices or assumptions that may create exclusive or unwelcome spaces for those we encounter in our communities.[98]

As we strip away the unhealthy parts of ourselves and our congregations, we experience resurrection into our true identities as reflections of God; we cannot stay mired in the guilt or shame of our idols or we will become paralyzed.[99] We must reawaken to God's image within (formation) so that we can share that icon of God with others (mission).

---

history to seek to be incorporated into the white culture. As a result, many people who consider themselves "white" have little connection to their ethnic roots.

95 For one starting point, see the metaphor of the "cultural flower" in Michelle Lebaron and Venashri Pillay, *Conflict across Cultures: A Unique Experience of Bridging Difference* (Boston: Intercultural, 2006), 48. See also Emmanuel Lartey's approach to intercultural pastoral care built around the assumption that each person is in some ways like all others, like some others, and like no others: *In Living Color: An Intercultural Approach to Pastoral Care and Counseling*, 2nd ed. (New York: Jessica Kingsley, 2003), 34.

96 There are many books available that explore differences in cultural orientation and values, including David Livermore, *Cultural Intelligence: Improving Your CQ to Engage Our Multicultural World* (Grand Rapids, MI: Baker Academic, 2009); Sarah A. Lanier, *Foreign to Familiar; A Guide to Understanding Hot- and Cold-Climate Cultures* (Hagerstown, MD: McDougal, 2000); and Mark Lau Branson and Juan F. Martinez, *Churches, Cultures, and Leadership: A Practical Theology of Congregations and Ethnicities* (Downers Grove, IL: IVP Academic, 2011).

97 David Augsburger suggests that crossing cultures includes sensitizing ourselves to the "common sense" of the Other while desensitizing ourselves to our own assumptions. *Conflict Mediation across Cultures* (Louisville, KY: Westminster/John Knox, 1992), 8–9.

98 Eric H. F. Law calls these our "boundary functions" in *Inclusion: Making Room for Grace* (St. Louis: Chalice, 2000), 15–27.

99 Eric H. F. Law, *The Wolf Shall Dwell with the Lamb: A Spirituality of Leadership in a Multicultural Community* (St. Louis: Chalice, 1993), 71–77.

Practice Three: Developing Mutual Friendships

God is already present in our neighborhoods and our world—we are not responsible for bringing God to those places or people.[100] We may find it difficult to recognize God in others from a distance, however; like living icons, we must contemplate them up close, over time.[101] While we cannot force relationship upon others, we can regularly position ourselves in places where relationships can be built—taking walks, engaging with neighborhood groups, establishing routines within our communities, and "practicing stability"[102] by making our homes permanent.[103]

As we begin to receive the gift of friendship from others, we can fight the instinct to control our relationships[104] and we can accept our need for others, even as we give of ourselves in return. Mutuality also involves extending hospitality as both a host and a guest and frequently sharing meals with those who are different from us.[105] As we develop friendships, we can cultivate curiosity about how and why our neighbors think and act the way they do and intentionally create a "grace margin," where we commit to discerning how we see God revealed in them without judgment.[106] As our love for our neighbors grows, we experience delight in our difference, celebrating the gift they bring to us and the world. This delight opens doors to remind others of the image of God in them: there is power in telling someone, "I see Jesus in you" or "I experienced God through you today." This is a missional act as we witness the Spirit reawakening our neighbors to the image of God they reflect.

People of Mission: *Being and Seeing Icons of God in the World*

These spiritual practices do not produce instant results; rather, they are entry points into the work of transformation. As we engage in these practices, we position ourselves to break old cycles of behavior and offer our consent to the transforming work of God's Spirit in and through us. All three practices are

---

100 See Thomas, "Anthropology, Mission, and the African Woman."

101 Ralph Servant, *Experiments in Love*, 125–26.

102 Alan Roxburgh and Martin Robinson, *Practices for the Refounding of God's People: The Missional Challenge of the West* (New York: Church Publishing, 2018), 151.

103 Many of these practices are embraced by the New Parish movement, as described by Paul Sparks, Tim Soerens, and Dwight J. Friesen in *The New Parish: How Neighborhood Churches Are Transforming Mission, Discipleship and Community* (Downers Grove, IL: IVP, 2014).

104 Welch, *Feminist Ethic*, 113.

105 Yong, *Hospitality and the Other*, 131–33; Safwat Marzouk, *Intercultural Church: A Biblical Vision for an Age of Migration* (Minneapolis: Fortress, 2019), 147–69.

106 Law, *Inclusion*, 45.

interrelated: (1) as we explore new narratives in Scripture, we begin to better recognize God in others; (2) as we recognize God in others, we are changed through new friendships so that we more clearly reflect a truer image of God; (3) as we shed the idols that have distorted the image of God in us, we encounter God in fresh ways and more clearly see God in our neighbors. Reflecting the image of God in the world by being transformed through the image of God in others is a long-term commitment, one that requires patience. Woodley reminds us that "conversion is both instantaneous and a process," and therefore we need to "think through those implications as we begin to consider our timelines. Then, throw out our timelines."[107]

Through the incarnation of Jesus—the perfect Icon of God—the image of God within us is reawakened and we participate in God's work of restoring the world. As we go about God's ministry of reconciliation, we encounter the image of God in others. When we consent to being transformed by those encounters, we reflect the image of God more fully so that, together, we can invite others into the Community of God. As we are formed into a people of mission, we expect to both *be* and *see* Icons of God in the world. May it be so.

107 Woodley, "Mission and the Cultural Other," 466.

Formation for Witness

Anabaptist Lessons Learned Far from Home

Robert Thiessen

Way back at the beginning, thirty-five years ago, I had no idea I could be a missionary. No one else thought I could be a missionary, either. I was a new believer (1986) attending the Mennonite Brethren (MB) church in Ontario I had grown up in and then rebelled from as an adolescent. The formation I received that first year was only indirectly about being a witness of God's love and more concerned with knowledge, conduct, and personal devotion. These were all good things, and, despite whatever may have been lacking, I am grateful for the leaders of those days. But I wanted more, not yet sure what that was. Then God opened the opportunity to go abroad.

By spring of 1988 I was living among rural Hondurans for a three-year apprenticeship that led to church-planting missions among the indigenous people of Mexico who were unreached by Christian missionaries.[1] The journey has been filled with mentors, disciplers, authors, and friends who formed me into an ambassador of God's Kingdom. This essay is a personal reflection on how this path helped me to identify increasingly as an Anabaptist, and how much of that came about despite my ethnic and religious background.

Honing Anabaptist Values in Northern Mexico

Thirty years ago, my wife, Anne, and I went to live high in the mountains of southern Mexico. Hundreds of thousands of pre-Columbian indigenous people survive there, far enough away from the aftermath of the Spanish Conquest to be left alone. When we first arrived, the isolation was extreme. In those days we'd hitch a ride to the village in a battered old stake truck along with a dozen locals and a handful of goats and chickens for company. We would stand for six hours, accumulating layers of chalky dust stirred up over the journey on harrowing roads that dropped off on either side for hundreds of feet into churn-

Robert Thiessen has served with Multiply, a Mennonite Brethren mission agency, among the indigenous peoples of Mexico since 1992. He and Anne are finishing their full-time ministry there and transitioning to serving the broader missions world from Ontario, Canada, in the areas of candidate training and interaction with indigenous populations.

1 The Roman Catholic church sent missionaries there in subsequent years.

ing rivers. Or we'd shiver in the relentless rain, wondering if the muddy tracks would prove too much for the bald tires.

Our invitation to spend the rainy summer in these mountains came from some locals we had met in northern Mexico in the agricultural fields of Sinaloa. They were part of the very first evangelical church in the entire region. None of the various North American mission agencies, including Wycliffe Bible Translators, had known they existed. Our research indicated that this was the area of Mexico most unreached by Christian missionaries, with no known believers and deep animism and steadfast resistance to outsiders. Yet time after time these were the people we were meeting in the migrant camps as we searched for where God was leading us. So we accepted the opportunity and pursued relationships and understanding and the Kingdom among this particular people group—the Metlatonoc Mixtecs—for the next fifteen years. It was among them that we honed our Anabaptist values as new leaders formed among the local people, but it was not where we first learned them.

My Anabaptist Formation Journey

I didn't learn much about Anabaptism as a young believer, even though I was raised in a Mennonite Brethren church. I deeply appreciate the leaders and friends of that era, and they are still my "home church"; however, very little of my experience then is what I now think of as distinctly Anabaptist. It was more akin to evangelicalism. In most ways, my upbringing and early formation were more Baptistic than anything else.

Perhaps this doesn't matter to most of the church. But for those of us who identify as Anabaptists, I think our ideology can bring a deeper spiritual witness and formation. Of particular importance to me is how we "do" cross-cultural missions when cultural "DNA" is often unwittingly exported. I believe the Anabaptist distinctives about the Kingdom of God, the centrality of Jesus, focused canon, shared leadership, community hermeneutic, and eschewing power can help us avoid many missteps. These are the areas that I believe identify our uniqueness.

Ironically, my formation as an Anabaptist started with a Baptist missionary, George Patterson, who mentored my mentor, another Baptist missionary. Patterson pioneered in the sixties and seventies what mission thinkers like Venn, Anderson, and Nevius had proposed a century earlier, and Roland Allen had called for in *Missionary Methods: St. Paul's or Ours* (1912).[2] These giants' ideas promoted local leadership that was fully capable of reproducing itself and of reflecting local cultural patterns and local abilities. Nevius, in *The Planting and*

2 Rolland Allen, *Missionary Methods: St. Paul's or Ours; A Study of the Church in the 4 Provinces* (London: Robert Scott, 1912).

Development of Missionary Churches (1899),[3] developed Venn and Anderson's ideas from thirty years previous into the idea of an indigenous church that is "self-governing, self-supporting, and self-propagating"—sometimes called the Three Selfs.

These concepts had begun to be implemented, haltingly and with much Western baggage, yet gaining traction. But by the end of the nineteenth century, a rising tide of reassertion of colonial pride eroded most of those advances. R. P. Beaver alludes to this: "Almost immediately after Venn's termination . . . (other leaders) took the view that the African was of inferior quality and could not provide ministerial leadership. . . . The African middle-class businessman and intellectual was despised. . . . Growing devotion to the theory of 'white man's burden' . . . reduced the native church to a colony of the foreign planting church."[4]

Ralph Winter further lays fault at the feet of the Student Volunteer Movement—the most influential group in missions from 1888, when it started among Princeton and Harvard students, until the inter-war period of the 1900s. He says that "the fresh new college students . . . did not always fathom how the older missionaries . . . could have turned responsibility over to national leaders at the least educated levels of society. . . . New [college-trained] missionaries . . . [who] assumed leadership over existing churches . . . in some cases . . . caused a huge step backward in mission strategy."[5] This renewed emphasis on the superiority of Western educational norms and forms had little space to value local leaders except to the extent that those leaders conformed to the expectations of Western academia and ideals.[6]

When Patterson went to Honduras to teach in a Bible College in the mid-sixties, the Three Self ideas of the previous century were nowhere to be found. He only knew one way of formation—the way most were doing it everywhere: find young men (the only ones free enough from family obligations) to attend the schools run by foreigners, subject them to two or more years of

---

3 John L. Nevius, *The Planting and Development of Missionary Churches* (New York: Foreign Mission Library, 1899).

4 R. Pierce Beaver, "The History of Mission Strategy," in *Perspectives on the World Christian Movement*, 3rd ed., ed. Stephen Hawthorne, (Pasadena: William Carey Library, 1999), 248–49.

5 Ralph Winter, "Four Men, Three Eras, Two Transitions," in *Perspectives on the World Christian Movement*, 3rd ed., ed. Stephen Hawthorne, (Pasadena: William Carey Library, 1999), 258.

6 I use "Western" and its variants to mean European peoples—including their colonial outposts—and all us descendants of them, who were formed by the Enlightenment, the protestant reformation and counter-reformation, and the scientific and industrial revolution.

rigorous learning (easily characterized as rote and narrow), instill patterns of spirituality the sending church was comfortable with (like private devotions, antiquated versions of the Bible, external forms of prayers and praise, three-point sermons), and then assign them to rule in churches made up of people older than themselves.

Patterson soon saw what so many others had seen as well—that this was a recipe for many types of problems. (*La fama, la dama, la lana* is a common Spanish refrain, meaning "fame, women, and money." It is a saying in church circles because so many young male pastors committed ethical violations in these areas.) He began to understand how these patterns hindered witness to God's goodness and Kingdom.

What makes him a pioneer, though, is that he changed things. Drastically. He shut the school down after two years of teaching there and began to work with middle-aged family men. He trained them in basic church practices that they could adapt, helping them find basic spiritual ideas in the Scriptures that they could ponder together. And, perhaps most importantly, he expected and gave them freedom to continue this formation with whomever God put in their path.

These new leaders, excited by the way Good News was transforming their lives, eagerly witnessed about their new faith in nearby villages to cousins, uncles, or friends. As soon as there was some response, they helped those people become new leaders in their own context. Patterson and all the subsequent regional leaders never kept power to themselves. In a distinct break from evangelical tradition, locals, who were not formally trained, led ordinances like baptism and communion. In twenty years, by the time I came on the scene, more than a hundred churches, all led by the locals, were utilizing their own resources and reproducing easily. Their holistic Kingdom witness and practice spread freely, unencumbered by outsiders. Just like Venn, Anderson, and Nevius had hoped for.

Here, promoted by a Baptist, the distinctives of focused canon, plural leadership, and community hermeneutic were forming church life, witness, and extension. Central to the Hondurans' ideology was simple obedience to Jesus Christ, and so the here-and-now Kingdom of God made up more of their life than any perception of themselves as participating in a Church Age with an other-worldly focus. Patterson, while remaining within his Baptist denomination, broke with many traditions (formal education requirements for leaders, titled pastor as primary congregational leader and teacher of Scripture, concentration on Pauline theology, dispensational perspective) and didn't use Anabaptist language, nor would any of those churches. His drive was to see churches born healthy, witnessing about the Kingdom and unhindered by baggage of their Western "parents." His relationship with locals and new readings of Scripture gave him the needed justification for such bold moves.

I didn't meet Patterson till after my three-year apprenticeship, when I was already engaged to his daughter, Anne. I have had the privilege of his insight and guidance for all these intervening years, till his death this past February 2022.

This training in Honduras began my formation as an Anabaptist, though I did not use that terminology. It gave me freedom to pursue a ministry of witness and formation among the indigenous people of Mexico who had not been reached by Christian missionaries.

I bring my experiences and opinions forward here not so much to promote Anabaptism as to encourage those of us who are Anabaptists to embrace our inherent strengths. The lessons Patterson learned in Honduras often opposed the patterns and theology of his denomination, and many of his struggles in implementing them were made more difficult by his background. Anabaptists have so much to draw on, and we don't have to "fight" our heritage and ideals; I could take to Mexico with me the Anabaptist values I learned in Honduras without being any less MB (in ideals if not in practice).

Applying Anabaptist Distinctives in Mexico

By the early nineties, Anne and I were starting life among the Mixtecs of Guerrero (and later, Oaxaca), where we sought to form local, plural, and untitled leaders that could reproduce their gifts in surrounding areas. We were focused on simple obedience to Jesus Christ, using a framework George Patterson had given us with Jesus at the center that included (1) the Three Levels of Authority—we obey Jesus always, we pay attention to Apostolic practice, we hold lightly to Church tradition—and (2) the Seven Commandments of Jesus, summarized as Repent and Believe, Baptize, Love, Give, Pray, Gather in Communion, and Disciple.[7] Living among the poorest people of Mexico at their socioeconomic level wasn't daunting, since Jesus, who gave up everything, was sending us there and we'd had some experience of living among the poor during our separate ministries in Honduras. Also, we were already comfortable with the *LAMP* (*Language Acquisition Made Practical*) approach to language learning developed by Tom and Elizabeth Brewster, which famously states: *Community Is My Classroom*. We prayed daily that God's Kingdom would come to earth as it is in heaven, and we acted accordingly.

Of course, and it does need saying, we made mistakes, had blind spots and baggage, could be petty or imperious, and had only begun our learning. We still do all of that. And following Anabaptist distinctives was no magic wand leading to significant growth. But along the way, as we applied Anabaptist dis-

7 George Patterson, "Spontaneous Multiplication of Churches," in *Perspectives on the World Christian Movement*, ed. Stephen Hawthorne, 3rd ed. (Pasadena: William Carey Library, 1999), 601.

tinctives (although we didn't call them that with the locals), we learned so much among the indigenous people.

For starters, we learned about animism, which, for the Mixtecs, meant that fear drove much of their behavior. As per their own assessment, shared with us as we tried to be good anthropologists not assuming anything from the start, we came to understand that theirs was a malevolent universe controlled by capricious spirits. The new believers constantly thanked Jesus for his power over those forces.

We also participated in communal living, where no party is complete without everyone present. We learned that, because of the village's efforts to equalize income, individual betterment wasn't necessarily a way out of poverty. This people group shared communal leadership, rotating elders in their villages through a somewhat democratic process that was initially adopted in the church as well.

And we had opportunities to see Scripture through non-Western eyes, realizing, for example, that the woman at the well in John 4 might not have been a "fallen" woman but a young girl treated poorly by the system around her, forced into an arranged marriage by age twelve and subsequently abandoned over and over. We began to interact with God's Word without reading it, through group discussions and storytelling, as we realized that no local believer would ever have private devotions utilizing the printed Word.

Watching peoples' lives redeemed and changed helped us see God's mercy much more widely than I had been raised to accept and also helped us understand that Divine initiative is the beginning of the story, not an add-in at the middle. The reading of Paul that concentrated on the end-point of salvation gave way to hearing him express how redemption also occurs along the way, as a journey.

We also had many opportunities to help other Westerners join this endeavor, both *anglo* North Americans and Mexican *Latinos*. The simplicity of initial training that formed life-long learning and witness was naturally reproduced with the apprentices that joined us. These fellow laborers then also passed on to others, from within their own resources and economies, what they had received (2 Tim 2:2).

Mennonite Brethren and Anabaptism: My Observations

Halfway through our time in Mexico (2003), we joined the mission agency of the Mennonite Brethren denomination in Canada and the United States. This is when I began to learn the language of Anabaptism. I had read Jacob Loewen and Paul Hiebert (famous missiologists with MB backgrounds), but neither really refers to Anabaptist distinctives. Loewen's last book, written in his seventies and after a stroke, was about being Anabaptist but not so much about missions, and he regrets not expounding on Anabaptism earlier. Hiebert (and Donald

McGavran) is known for the "Fourth Self," that of self-theologizing—encouraging contextualization and new expressions of the church. That perhaps corresponds to the Community Hermeneutic distinctive, but I am not aware that he identifies it as such.

These two thinkers are highly esteemed by fellow missiologists of their era and continue to significantly influence the field of missiology.[8] They both call for much the same things I outline here but without appealing to the built-in strengths of their theological family. I believe this highlights again that much has been eroded in we who identify as Evangelical Anabaptists. Like Patterson, they too "flew in the face" of established patterns, but they shouldn't have had to.

Through conversations with various agency and denominational leaders (including international ones), and some related readings, I came to understand that the missiological ideas I was discovering were supposed to be central to the whole Anabaptist endeavor. These people helped me understand this better, but I found only limited real-life applications. Unfortunately, our Mennonite Brethren family does not always adhere to its own Anabaptist roots.[9] For example:

- Our mission agency still requires postsecondary formal study (with some exceptions).
- We still have trouble living Incarnationally in poor fields (not so hard in Europe but more so in America, Africa, and Asia).
- We still, thankfully less and less, restrict the leadership of rites like baptism and communion to the "ordained," but even in our newest endeavors there are leaders borrowed from other denominations who make it difficult for new believers to share in leading these basic activities.
- We still encourage private devotions focused on reading the Bible and journaling—practices that are difficult for much of the rest of the world. By default, the missionary receives little practice of devotional habits useful for discipling communal and oral people.
- We still tend to form pastors instead of elders. We still tend to send them to institutes of higher learning (less high as we try to adapt) to become so titled.
- We still expect these "pastors" to preach with little consultation within their communities, and we still send our dollars so that this can happen in "*templos*" or whatever the set-aside places of worship get called.

8 See the introduction to Jacob Loewen's *Culture and Human Values: Christian Intervention in Anthropological Perspective; Selections from the Writings of Jacob A. Loewen* (South Pasadena, CA: William Carey Library, 2000).

9 Despite my critique in this section, we are a great group of dedicated and sacrificial servants, and I am glad to serve in this agency.

Within our agency we have widely differing understanding around these things. What is striking, though, is how little we appeal to our Anabaptist beginnings. Although there is some level of recognition that these patterns I identify are problematic, many do not regret how we do things. We have a couple of great books that point us differently (*Global Church Planting* by Ott and Wilson,[10] for one) that the agency recommends, but field practitioners rarely read them. We have strategy maps and vision statements that should guide us more clearly. We have good people all over the globe, most of whom want things to be different but are constrained by inertia, patterns, expectations, and existing molds.

On the other hand, we have grown over the decades, and some things that used to be normal aren't anymore: We used to expect new missionaries to have postgraduate formal education; now it is only postsecondary. There are far fewer cases of restricted leadership, and we're a little less likely to use titles (but in honor cultures, that value is easily eroded). We throw around a lot less money and other resources than we used to. We're better about sending servant leaders that function under (and never more than beside) local leaders. But somehow we still get maneuvered into too many situations where the "white" outsider has outsized influence. We often don't know how to resist that.

My exposure to the rest of the Anabaptist world is limited, mostly to other groups that identify as Evangelical Anabaptists. I've not seen or heard that their practices around this are much different. We all seem to suffer from the same malady of syncretism, the Westernization of the church (admittedly started a long time ago, long before Menno Simons walked the earth). And our formation to be witnesses of God's Kingdom is much more evangelical than Anabaptist.

Anabaptist Distinctives: Foundation for Best Practices

I propose we further develop theology and practices that strengthen our capacity to be Kingdom ambassadors. We could overtly draw on our Anabaptist distinctives as foundation for missiological "best practices," teaching new missionaries to work from our strengths. We could have fully field-based apprenticeships that emphasize Incarnational living, group faith-building practices, communal elder leadership, and simplicity in requirements and patterns. We could offer rigorous guidance in avoiding the many and common pitfalls Westerners face because our default position as privileged is so ingrained, widespread, and strong.

I reflect here, and offer my opinion, with the hope and prayer that we all will welcome conversations with anyone in our church family (Anabaptist or

10 Craig Ott and Gene Wilson, *Global Church Planting: Biblical Principals and Best Practices for Multiplication* (Grand Rapids, MI: Baker Academic, 2011).

otherwise) who wants to pursue a community hermeneutic around pathways that embrace our heritage, our ideas, and our possibilities.

I write this as well for people like the Mixtecs, wherever they are "hiding" all over the globe, evading the effects of colonization. Anabaptist witness, which so easily can hinder, has even greater possibility for good when it joins with indigenous peoples to discover the freest and fullest pathway in the Kingdom that God wants for us all.

Mission as Distraction?

A Critical Twist on Formation and Mission in Anabaptist Communities on the Möbius Loop

Sarah Ann Bixler

Ring of Möbius **by Hans Kalkhoven, Eindhoven University of Technology, Eindhoven, the Netherlands, 1986.**

A physical möbius strip made by the author.

Church on the Möbius Loop

Imagine a long, thin strip of paper with different colors—red and yellow—on either side. Now imagine this strip of paper lying straight on a flat surface, with its red side visible and yellow side face down. You pick up the strip by its ends, then turn one end over so that you can now see the red side on one half of your twisted strip and the yellow side on the other. You bring your hands together, laying the yellow end on top of the opposite red end. You secure the ends together with a piece of tape, and you have a Möbius loop.

Sarah Ann Bixler (PhD, Princeton Theological Seminary) is Assistant Professor of Formation and Practical Theology, and Associate Dean at Eastern Mennonite Seminary in Harrisonburg, VA.

The Möbius loop is a well-known mathematical puzzle, fascinating to artists and engineers alike. With its curious characteristics, it is the subject of two M. C. Escher works as well as a design for machine belts and typewriter ribbons.[1] The Möbius loop consists of a surface with only one side—an object that cannot be oriented up or down, back or front, side to side. You can trace your finger along its single surface forever, without falling off an edge. As you do so, the wear is even on both sides.

In *A Hidden Wholeness*, Parker Palmer writes about "life on the Möbius strip" to illustrate the integration between a person's inner life and outer life. "Whatever is inside of us continually flows outward to help form, or deform, the world," Palmer explains, "and whatever is outside us continually flows inward to help to form, or deform, our lives."[2] Bit by bit, we and our world are endlessly re-made in this perpetual inner-outer exchange. Palmer takes the message of the Möbius loop to highlight the absence of a discernable inner or outer surface, such that the two co-create each other.

As I think about the dimensions of Anabaptist witness, I find the Möbius loop to be an apt metaphor. It illustrates the integral relationship between the church's inner and outer lives, reminding the church of what it means to have integrity. The words *integration* and *integrity* come from the same Latin root meaning "whole." The church can experience wholeness in its inner and outer realities when formation and witness are part of an unorientable whole, like the Möbius loop. This, I believe, is what it means for the church to have missional integrity.

The two sides of the Möbius loop are correlated with faith metaphors in a variety of ways. Palmer, from the reference point of the individual person, speaks of the inward and outward dimensions of life. More relevant to our present consideration, my former professors Bo Karen Lee and Richard Osmer identify the two aspects of ecclesiology as spirituality and mission, or the dual calls to follow Christ and serve the world.[3] Osmer bases this ecclesiological formulation on the Barthian upbuilding and sending functions of the church.[4] Lee and Osmer call for nurturing both the church's inner life in Christ—what they

---

1 The Dutch artist M. C. Escher created two woodcuts of this image: *Mobius Strip I* in 1961 and *Mobius Strip II* in 1963. See https://www.nga.gov/collection/art-object-page.61283.html and https://www.nga.gov/collection/art-object-page.61286.html.

2 Parker J. Palmer, *A Hidden Wholeness: The Journey toward an Undivided Life* (San Francisco, CA: Jossey-Bass, 2008), 47.

3 Bo Karen Lee, "The 'Double-Pointed Ellipse:' Integrating Spirituality and Mission," in *Consensus and Conflict: Practical Theology for Congregations in the Work of Richard R. Osmer*, ed. Kenda Creasy Dean et al. (Eugene, OR: Pickwick, 2019), 93.

4 Richard R. Osmer, "Formation in the Missional Church: Building Deep Connections between Ministries of Upbuilding and Sending," in *Cultivating Sent Communities:*

term "spirituality"—and the church's outer life of mission, so that the church's formation has both a spiritual and missional character.[5]

Instead of "spirituality" and "mission," I am choosing to use the similar terms "formation" and "witness" to correlate with the two colors that comprise the Möbius loop. In a study called the Missional Leadership Project, pastoral leaders used the language of formation "to describe the ways a congregation shapes the lives of its members and builds up the 'culture' of a particular congregation."[6] From this perspective, formation is a human endeavor, the effect of a group on individuals and the emergence of a common culture. In contrast, Osmer argues that the Holy Spirit is the primary actor in Christian formation, with human-driven formation being secondary.[7]

I affirm Osmer's perspective as the ideal. Yet, formation by God's Spirit largely depends on the community opening itself to being changed by the movement of God among them. In reality, I believe our churches are formed by more human factors than we might want to acknowledge. Cultural shifts and internal conflict exert pressure on communities to abandon or reinforce existing behaviors and commitments, and in these moments of intense emotional anxiety it is difficult to attend to the Spirit's guidance. When the Holy Spirit is the primary actor in Christian formation, wise leadership responses have a prophetic and pastoral quality that builds up the spirituality of the community, rather than a reactive quality that deforms the community.

On the other side of the Möbius loop from formation we have witness. By witness, I mean the communication—through being, saying, and doing—of one's beliefs and values.[8] In the case of Anabaptist witness, I envision this as the communication of the gospel of Jesus Christ to persons both within and outside of an Anabaptist community. (I will elaborate on this further later in this article.) Yet, it is important to recognize that even in naming the two colors in the Möbius loop as distinct identities, we must uphold the seamless transition between the two; when the church engages in witness it will suddenly find itself being formed in that act.[9] Likewise, as the church is seeking to be formed by God's Spirit, it will find itself being called outside of itself to engage in acts of

---

Missional Spiritual Formation, ed. Dwight J. Zscheile, Missional Church Series (Grand Rapids, MI: Eerdmans, 2012), 52.

5 Lee, "The 'Double-Pointed Ellipse:' Integrating Spirituality and Mission," 97.

6 Osmer, "Formation in the Missional Church," 33.

7 Osmer, 49.

8 Darrell L. Guder, *Be My Witnesses: The Church's Mission, Message, and Messengers* (Grand Rapids, MI: Eerdmans, 1985).

9 Osmer, "Formation in the Missional Church," 51. Osmer writes, "The congregation and its members are *formed* as they act with and for others beyond the church in partnership, mutual learning, and solidarity with the vulnerable."

witness. The two are experienced in a continuing loop, existing with integrity as two parts of a whole.

Interestingly, Lee and Osmer's spirituality-mission framework stems from a Möbius-like relation developed by Winston Crum. Crum's 1973 description of the mathematical metaphor of the ellipse is as follows:

> The church is rather like an ellipse, having two foci. In and around the first she acknowledges and enjoys the Source of her life and mission. This is an ingathering and recharging focus. Worship and prayer are emphasized here. From and through the other focus she engages and challenges the world. This is a forth-going and self-spending focus. Service and evangelization are stressed. Ideally, Christians learn to function in both ways at once, as it were making the ellipse into a circle with both foci at the center.[10]

A two-dimensional ellipse looks like an oval, with a center point and two points equidistant from the center that serve as dual focal points. Crum identifies one focal point as having the purpose of ingathering and recharging, marked by the practices of worship and prayer. The second focal point's purpose is going forth and spending one's self in the practices of service and evangelization. Crum calls for these two movements to occur simultaneously, so that both merge as a single central focus, which turns the oval-shaped, two-foci ellipse into a circle with a single centerpoint and no other distinct foci. When missiologist David Bosch picks up Crum's metaphor of the ellipse-turned-circle, he adds, "Neither focus should ever be at the expense of the other; rather, they stand in each other's service."[11] In this way, Bosch highlights the retained identities of ingathering and forthgoing that Crum alludes to, even as they shift into a single centerpoint.

A Critical Twist

Revisiting our imagined exercise that opened this essay, we can recognize that a Möbius loop would essentially be an ellipse if it were not for a single important motion—a twist. This critical motion is the twisting of one end of the strip of paper before securing both ends together. An important contribution of the Möbius metaphor, then, is the seamless continuity that also allows the two sides of the strip to retain their distinctiveness. This distinctiveness becomes obscured in Crum's ellipse. While we must acknowledge the limitations of any metaphor, the consequence of Crum's ellipse-turned-circle is that the two foci

---

10 Winston F. Crum, "The Missio Dei and the Church: An Anglican Perspective," *St. Vladimir's Theological Quarterly* 17, no. 4 (1973): 288.

11 David Jacobus Bosch, *Transforming Mission: Paradigm Shifts in Theology of Mission*, Twentieth anniversary ed, American Society of Missiology Series 16 (Maryknoll, NY: Orbis, 2011), 385.

blend together as the shape transforms into a circle. In the Möbius loop, however, there is integration *and* distinction. I therefore advocate for an integration that retains distinction—an integration without erasure or eclipse.[12] The red and yellow sides do not become orange; they maintain their original character within a new, integrated whole. In the Möbius loop metaphor for conceptualizing formation and witness, one twist makes all the difference. I propose this twist as "critical" in two senses of the word: 1) as a critique of reductionist patterns of Anabaptist witness, and 2) as an essential element—that is, a crucial or vital part—of Anabaptist witness.

It is a common impulse in Anabaptist thought to fuse the ingathering and forthgoing foci, or, as I am identifying them, formation and witness. Among John Howard Yoder's many influences on Anabaptist thought that I find problematic is his conceptualization of the inner and outer dimensions of the church as a single reality—collapsing rather than integrating them.[13] When Yoder defines the church as a political entity, he equates the inner life of the body of Christ with its witness to "the watching world."[14] Approaching this type of equation from both directions, C. Norman Kraus argues, "The life of the church *is* its witness. The witness of the church *is* its life. The question of authentic witness is the question of authentic community."[15] Yet when the inner life of the church is conceptualized as its witness, dynamics of power and the realities of social inequality can be too easily dismissed in light of a pure religious vision.

---

12 My perspective is informed by the logic of Deborah van Deusen Hunsinger's application of Barth's Chalcedonian pattern, where two concepts exist in a relation "without separation or division [unity], without confusion or change [differentiation], and with the conceptual priority of theology over psychology [order]." I am drawing from the first aspect of this pattern; I depart from Hunsinger's framework in my assumption that one aspect can indeed change the other and that there is no inherent theological priority of one over the other. See Deborah van Deusen Hunsinger, *Theology and Pastoral Counseling: A New Interdisciplinary Approach* (Grand Rapids, MI: Eerdmans, 1995), 10.

13 Yoder, *Body Politics: Five Practices of the Christian Community Before the Watching World* (Scottdale, PA: Herald, 2001), 74–75. In addition to concerns I have with Yoder's thought and practice, not least of which is his sexual abuse of dozens of women, I question the extent of his assumption of a watching world in *Body Politics*. Well into the twenty-first century as we are, to continue claiming the wider world as "a subset of the world vision of the gospel" glosses over the lived reality of many people for whom the theological meaning of Christian practices is not immediately apparent. Distinctive practices like intercultural fellowship, sharing food, and extending forgiveness do not belong to Christians alone, and many who claim the Christian label fail to practice them.

14 Yoder, ix.

15 C. Norman Kraus, *The Authentic Witness: Credibility and Authority* (Grand Rapids, MI: Eerdmans, 1978), 156.

Here, it also becomes important to recognize that even inner-outer distinctions are misleading. Formation does not happen only within the church; as I stated above, we are formed by God's Spirit in the act of witness in interaction with persons outside of the covenanted faith community. Moreover, the entity Yoder takes to be "the world" is not the only audience that may be watching. People also watch from within—those who have not yet committed to membership in the believer's church. This includes persons who come to Anabaptism through theological seeking or are drawn by its practices of community, and young people who attend with families and friends, engaging in what Jean Lave and Etienne Wenger call "legitimate peripheral participation."[16] The Möbius loop reminds us that when we think we are dealing in formation, without warning we find ourselves in the midst of witness, and when we think we are enacting witness, we find that God is at work forming us. Smooth shifting from one dimension into the other occurs continuously.

The relationship between formation and witness, though not necessarily in those particular terms, is a conundrum addressed by many Christian scholars. In the quasi-Anabaptist Quaker tradition, Parker Palmer wants to integrate the inward-outward dimensions of life to the extent that they form only one reality.[17] Womanist ethicist Emilie Townes makes a compelling case for integrating faith and life, what appears to be collapsing witness into spiritual formation as the subtitle of her book would suggest: *Womanist Spirituality as Social Witness*. She identifies her womanist spirituality as self-critical and reflective, vital, and demanding.[18] Yet, Townes's integration is more nuanced than Yoder's collapse, as the result of her spiritual formation is to live a more robust social witness "that involves the skills of social analysis, theological and biblical reflection, ethical examination, and mother wit" as the intersecting oppressions in the Black community are examined and challenged.[19] One impacts the other, and therein lies their inseparability.

I find the collapsing of formation and witness and, relatedly, the inner and outer life of the church, to be an inadequate model for Anabaptist witness. When we collapse formation and witness into one another, either can become lost or overlooked in our theology and practice. I appreciate the way Anabaptist

---

16 Jean Lave and Etienne Wenger, *Situated Learning: Legitimate Peripheral Participation*, Learning in Doing (New York: Cambridge University Press, 1991). One of my colleagues, Kate Unruh, is exploring legitimate peripheral participation as a framework for young people's Christian formation in her forthcoming 2022 dissertation at Princeton Theological Seminary.

17 Palmer, *A Hidden Wholeness*, 47.

18 Emilie Maureen Townes, *In a Blaze of Glory: Womanist Spirituality as Social Witness* (Nashville: Abingdon, 1995), 122.

19 Townes, 13.

missional theologian Robert J. Suderman claims being and doing as two critical, inseparable entities. He articulates a missional vision for the church as "the formation of a people, *transformed by the loving sacrifice of Jesus Christ, the Son of God, and sent into the world as an agent of the reconciliation willed by God*."[20] For Suderman, Anabaptist witness entails both a formative being and a transformational doing, and they are neither collapsible nor inseparable. He continues, "The agenda of *being is foundational to the agenda of doing*, and the agenda of *doing is indispensable to the agenda of being*."[21] Such careful attentiveness to both sides of the Möbius loop is important for the church's integrity, and they exist in a dynamic interrelation rather than as an equatedness or one-directional cause and effect.

Undoubtedly, the church's inner life bears witness both to persons within the church and beyond it. Our core values and beliefs are revealed most authentically in what we do rather than what we say. Yet, when this leads us to simply collapse witness into formation, we turn our focus solely to the inner life of the church and disrupt the Möbius flow of formation and witness.

A collapse leads to conclusions like the common sentiment I heard expressed in a Mennonite Sunday school session: "If I live my life right, I trust people will take notice and recognize there's something different about me because I'm a Christian."[22] This is like Yoder's assumption, substituting the inner life for witness, living as the quiet in the land. This is neither consistent with the ministry of Jesus and his disciples nor with the apostolic mission of Paul. The gospel demands not merely a quiet life lived rightly but intentional engagement with persons inside and outside the faith community in order to call and act for God's justice and reconciliation, while also communicating the motivation and meaning of these words and actions. Formation in the inner life of the church is incomplete without witness, and witness is hollow without the deep resources of formation. As Bosch and others remind us, the faithful church has a double focus—both inward and outward—on formation and witness.[23]

Anabaptist missional theologian Lois Barrett argues against these divisions between the gospel as outreach or nurture, being or doing, and evangelism or congregational life. She instead advocates for a holistic approach whereby "the community's thought, words, and deeds are being formed into a pattern that proclaims the gospel of the crucified and risen Jesus Christ. As a result, the good news of God's reign is publicly announced. The proclamation is a 'word

20 Robert J Suderman, *Re-Imagining the Church: Implications of Being a People in the World*, ed. Andrew G. Suderman (Eugene, OR: Wipf & Stock, 2016), 47.

21 Suderman, 48.

22 Coincidentally, I heard this comment in an LMC congregation in 2019.

23 Bosch, *Transforming Mission*, 385.

and deed' proclamation; it is not only audible but visible as well."[24] In this way, Barrett envisions the missional church as identifiable in its character, which is made manifest as "the missional church both *proclaims the gospel and embodies the gospel.*"[25] She thus envisions missional congregations that embody the gospel in a way that makes inner and outer congruent, not just connected.[26]

Formation and Witness in LMC: A Fellowship of Anabaptist Churches

In contrast to this congruency approach illustrated by the Möbius loop, the ease with which Anabaptists may assume the formation-as-witness posture sometimes manifests itself in the inverse—witness-as-formation. This is the opposite distortion of focus that violates the Möbius loop principle I am proposing. When this occurs, instead of collapsing witness into formation, formation is eclipsed by witness, ignored in light of a laser-bright focus on witness.

I have observed indicators of this witness-as-formation posture in one regional Mennonite conference's navigation of the conflict plaguing the inner life of Mennonite Church USA (MC USA). People who are watching, both from without and within, question the integrity of a peace church's witness when its own members cannot stand to be with one another and are embroiled in disagreement, hostility, and plays for power over one another. Importantly, in his 1976 book *Community and Commitment*, John Driver places his chapter on a community of peace before his chapter on being a missionary community. "The very forms of the church's obedience constituted a powerful missionary witness," he explains.[27] For Driver, in the Anabaptist Mennonite tradition peace is experienced as "social relationships characterized by justice" and living together in harmony with God and one another.[28] He concludes, "The true criterion for evaluating our evangelistic practices is the formation of disciple communities obedient to Jesus."[29] On the one hand, outward witness is absolutely affected by the church's inner life; and on the other hand, ecclesiology becomes reductionist if inner formation becomes the primary focus of the church.

---

24 Lois Y. Barrett, ed., "Embodying and Proclaiming the Gospel," in *Treasure in Clay Jars: Patterns in Missional Faithfulness*, ed. Lois Barrett, The Gospel and Our Culture Series (Grand Rapids, MI: Eerdmans, 2004), 149.

25 Barrett, 151.

26 Barrett, 153.

27 John Driver, *Community and Commitment*, Mission Forum Series 4 (Scottdale, PA: Herald, 1976), 81.

28 Driver, 70.

29 Driver, 92.

I will now turn to a specific case in which one side of the Möbius loop—outward witness—is emphasized as a strategy for detracting attention from the church's inner life. This is what I identify as using mission as distraction, which I observe in recent leadership strategies of LMC: A Fellowship of Anabaptist Churches, formerly known as Lancaster Mennonite Conference.

As conflict ensued over developments in MC USA, a growing impulse arose for LMC to emphasize mission in language, energy, resources, and branding, which I interpret as both an implicit and explicit strategy to eclipse the presence of conflict within the inner life of the church. In my description of events that follows, I am not suggesting that LMC is the only Anabaptist entity where this strategy is evident or even where it is the most acute, or that this is the only conflict response that LMC leaders have offered. All ecclesial situations are complex, and I do not wish to be reductive in my analysis. Yet, my recent position as a dual member of LMC and MC USA has afforded me proximity to processes, documents, presentations, and leaders' reflections where I have seen a witness-as-formation posture. Exploring LMC as an Anabaptist community in light of formation and witness invites us deeper into concrete practical theological reflection, which is my aim in this article.

LMC has its roots in the Swiss-German Mennonite migration to southeastern Pennsylvania of the early eighteenth century. These descendants of religious refugees established farmsteads and met for worship in homes and meetinghouses scattered throughout Lancaster County.[30] By 1820, a regional district conference had emerged.[31] By the end of the nineteenth century, mission efforts arose with the Home Mission Advocates, the forerunner of Eastern Mennonite Board of Missions and Charities (EMM) that was established in 1914 and remains highly active today.[32] Throughout the twentieth century, EMM initiated mission efforts in over fifty countries on six continents, motivated by what A. Grace Wenger in her EMM centennial history book calls "compassion for the poor and hungry."[33] At this 100-year mark, EMM estimated that church-

---

30 I wish to acknowledge one line of power in which I live in proximity to this community. My ancestor Hans Herr was the first Mennonite bishop to immigrate to Pennsylvania. He, along with six other Swiss Mennonite men, purchased ten thousand acres in Lancaster County in 1710 to form the first Mennonite settlement in Lancaster County.

31 L. Keith Weaver, "History of Mennonite General Conference," unpublished paper, obtained October 9, 2015.

32 Henry F. Garber, "Eastern Mennonite Missions (Lancaster Mennonite Conference)," *Global Anabaptist Mennonite Encyclopedia Online*, 1955, accessed March 8, 2022. https://gameo.org/index.php?title=Eastern_Mennonite_Missions_(Lancaster_Mennonite_Conference)&oldid=169413.

33 A. Grace Wenger, *A People in Mission: 1894–1994* (Salunga, PA: Eastern Mennonite Missions, 1994), 14.

es planted by EMM missionaries beyond North American annually "are now baptizing as many members as there are in Lancaster Mennonite Conference."[34] Meanwhile, within the United States LMC expanded beyond its European American membership and gained more diversity as African American, Southeast Asian, and Latinx individuals and congregations joined the conference. Yet, even as LMC engaged in mission and outreach, internal conflict marked these Anabaptists' story for over three centuries as congregations exercised the ban and separated from one another. A 2010 report, for instance, documents twenty-eight different Anabaptist ecclesial groups residing in Lancaster County.[35]

LMC currently operates with a self-governing system of district bishops who supervise pastoral leaders and congregations within the conference and serve on its Bishop Board.[36] The Bishop Board appoints a Conference Executive Council as the official governing body of the conference, which, in practice, shares governance with the Conference Leadership Assembly consisting of all credentialed leaders. It is the Bishop Board, however, that holds the power to ratify and revise the LMC Constitution. It has even overturned decisions of the Conference Leadership Assembly; for instance, in January 2007 the Conference Leadership Assembly failed by four votes to affirm the Bishop Board's recommendation to ordain women for ministry and pastoral leadership.[37] In May 2008, the Bishop Board overrode this vote by granting congregations the autonomy to ordain women.[38] In December 2021, the Bishop Board decided to "acknowledge and affirm that space has been created within LMC for women to serve on Bishop Oversight Teams," recognizing that Hyacinth Banks Stevens had been serving as part of the New York bishop team since 2016. The decision stops short of allowing women to serve as the leading bishop of a district.[39]

As one of the oldest Mennonite enclaves in the United States, LMC has used its membership status to exercise influence while retaining autonomy in relation

---

34 Wenger, 15.

35 C. Nelson Hostetter, "Lancaster, PA, City/County Anabaptist Groups," (Lititz, PA: May 12, 2010), accessed December 17, 2015, https://mennonitelife.org/document/pa-stats-2010-05-12-2/.

36 "Constitution of the Lancaster Mennonite Conference," Lancaster Mennonite Conference, September 2000.

37 Keith Weaver, "Ordination of Women Vote Results," January 19, 2007, accessed February 11, 2022, email to LMC leaders, https://lmcchurches.org/wp-content/uploads/2017/05/4.15-Ordination-of-Women-Vote-Results.pdf.

38 Celeste Kennel-Shank, "Lancaster Conference to Allow Ordination of Women for the First Time," *Mennonite Weekly Review*, June 2, 2008.

39 Paul Schrag, "LMC Lifts Ban on Women Bishops," *Anabaptist World*, February 4, 2022, accessed February 11, 2022. https://anabaptistworld.org/lmc-lifts-ban-on-women-bishops/.

to national Mennonite bodies with which it has affiliated over the years. For instance, when the Mennonite General Conference was created in 1898 as the first official Mennonite advisory body in the United States, LMC participated in it but never formally joined. Again, when the Mennonite Church reorganized in 1971, LMC resisted joining and instead participated without a formal vote.[40] After the 2001 merger of the General Conference Mennonite and Mennonite Churches that created MC USA, LMC operated under provisional membership status until 2004, when it joined as the largest of twenty-one area conferences of MC USA. By this time, however, it had lost about one-third of its congregations over the internal controversy about joining the denomination.[41]

After joining MC USA, LMC found itself in the uncomfortable position of lacking control over other conferences and congregations with whom it was affiliated across the national church. When LMC tried to hold other conferences accountable to specific aspects of *The Confession of Faith in a Mennonite Perspective (1995)*[42] and the denomination's Membership Guidelines, it met resistance. In 2013, LMC entered a two-year process to reassess its affiliation with MC USA. Increasing instances of Mennonite pastors in same-sex relationships, without discipline from MC USA leadership, frustrated many LMC leaders and members. A July 2014 survey found that nearly two-thirds of LMC credentialed leaders held serious concerns about LMC's membership in MC USA.[43] LMC's Board of Bishops sought feedback by holding regional "listening and vision casting meetings" across the conference during the summer of 2015. The contentious decade of membership in MC USA was brought to an end in November of that year, when 82 percent of LMC's credentialed leaders passed the bishops' proposal to withdraw from MC USA.[44] L. Keith Weaver, moderator of LMC since 2000, lamented at the end of the process, "Ever since [2000] we've been steeped in controversy and conflict."[45] Relationships within the con-

40 Weaver, "History of Mennonite General Conference."

41 "Lancaster Mennonite Conference Leaders Vote to Leave MCUSA," *The Mennonite*, November 19, 2015, https://anabaptistworld.org/lancaster-mennonite-conference-leaders-vote-to-leave-mcusa/. When it began withdrawal in 2015, LMC was still the largest conference of MC USA, with LMC's 13,838 members in 163 congregations.

42 General Conference Mennonite Church and Mennonite Church, *The Confession of Faith in a Mennonite Perspective* (Scottdale, PA: Herald, 1995).

43 "(Regional) Listening and Vision Casting Meetings," booklet, Lancaster Mennonite Conference, August 11, 2015, 15.

44 "Lancaster Mennonite Conference Leaders Vote to Leave MCUSA."

45 Personal interview with L. Keith Weaver, September 23, 2015. I am grateful to L. Keith Weaver, LMC moderator, for granting me a personal interview that informs much of this article, and for clarifying what I have perceived through personal connections in LMC. I grew up as a teenager in LMC and was baptized into membership in 1992

ference were stretched to the breaking point, and the inner life of the conference was shaken.

Mission as Distraction?

LMC called its process of assessing denominational affiliation "listening and vision casting."[46] While the presenting problem of same-sex relationships provided the impetus for reassessing affiliation, LMC introduced the conversation in the context of its 2020 Vision and "the missional call of God." Throughout an informational booklet to prepare attendees for these listening and vision casting meetings, the focus shifts back and forth between a commitment to heterosexual marriage and a missional approach. In this way, LMC leveraged its theological commitment to mission as an alternative to the internal conflict over same-sex marriage. Rhetoric expressing a church-world duality fuels this mission-refocusing strategy. The booklet states, "Worldly pressures threaten to undermine our faith. We are all quite aware of the rapid changes occurring in the culture around us. Few things give evidence of this change more clearly than changing attitudes about same-sex relationships."[47]

This dualistic impulse was echoed in the listening and vision-casting meetings themselves. One member asserted in a public forum, "We need to separate from people who think differently than us."[48] The booklet cites survey data gauging leaders' positions on homosexual practice, which were overwhelmingly negative.[49] This same survey also revealed positive interest in mission-related activities: church revitalization, church planting, congregational multiplication initiatives, and aid for local communities. The booklet concludes, "These survey results confirm that LMC congregations are taking the missional call of God very seriously."[50] Mission is thus presented as a positive alternative to the negative energy around the internal conflict.

As LMC departed from MC USA in 2015, it employed a strategy to shift the focus from the inner life of the church to its outer activity of mission. This is not the first time LMC has used its theological commitment to mission as a

---

in an LMC congregation pastored by my father. While holding primary membership in Virginia Mennonite Conference congregations from 2001 to the present, I most recently had associate membership from 2014 to 2019 at an LMC congregation in Philadelphia.

46 "(Regional) Listening and Vision Casting Meetings."

47 "(Regional) Listening and Vision Casting Meetings."

48 Regional Listening and Vision Casting Meeting, Lancaster Mennonite Conference, Elizabethtown Mennonite Church, Elizabethtown, PA, August 27, 2015.

49 According to the survey, "82.7% of LMC leaders do not affirm homosexual practice," "(Regional) Listening and Vision Casting Meetings."

50 "(Regional) Listening and Vision Casting Meetings."

distraction from conflict with the broader church, rallying remaining congregations around the activity of witness. In *Latino Mennonites: Civil Rights, Faith, and Evangelical Culture*, Felipe Hinojosa reports that in 1970 LMC influenced Latino members to create their own Council of Spanish Mennonite Churches rather than join the national Minority Ministries Council (MMC) of the Mennonite church, which LMC perceived as focused on political and church reform. Hinojosa writes, "Under the direction of the mostly conservative Lancaster Mennonite Conference, the majority of Puerto Rican congregations in New York City were openly discouraged from working with or joining the MMC." Notably, in contrast to the MMC, the LMC council focused on evangelism and church planting. This illustrates the strategy to emphasize missional endeavors rather than engage internal concerns, in this case a movement for racial and social justice within the church.[51] Moreover, Moderator Weaver interprets LMC's 2015 withdrawal in terms of mission, citing the parting of Paul and Barnabas even as they served the same greater mission (Acts 15:36–41). As for LMC's relationship with MC USA, Weaver says he hopes "by God's grace, that rather than . . . leave all kinds of trails of pain, we can make space for each other and maintain collaboration for the shared mission of God."[52] As LMC severed its conflictual relationship with MC USA, it concomitantly articulated a hope for a greater mission.

By reshaping the narrative of internal conflict in terms of a missional vision, Weaver seeks to use the conflict as a way to propel the conference forward. He believes the process of withdrawing from MC USA "is productive pain; something is being birthed here."[53] Weaver describes local missional effectiveness, the impacting of neighborhoods, and the church's recovery of the healing ministries of Christ as signs of hope in the midst of crisis. In March 2018, Weaver announced the approval of a new name for the conference and presented the rationale to rebrand as LMC: A Fellowship of Anabaptist Churches. The rebranding primarily emphasized geography, though Weaver also acknowledged LMC's desire to retain its Mennonite identity.[54] LMC now uses the tagline "We empower congregations in the mission of God" and initially described itself as "an expanding fellowship of Anabaptist congregations proclaiming Christ to all peoples."[55] Indeed, LMC is rapidly expanding; the membership boundaries

---

51 Felipe Hinojosa, *Latino Mennonites: Civil Rights, Faith, and Evangelical Culture* (Baltimore: Johns Hopkins University Press, 2014), 119.

52 Interview with Weaver.

53 Interview with Weaver.

54 Rachel Stella, "Lancaster Conference Begins New Era," *Mennonite World Review*, April 2, 2018, https://anabaptistworld.org/lancaster-conference-begins-new-era/.

55 "LMC—A Fellowship of Anabaptist Churches," accessed October 31, 2019 and December 3, 2021, https://lmcchurches.org/.

of the conference are pushed well beyond the Northeastern United States, extending to the Dominican Republic and Nicaragua.

When I view LMC's turn toward mission from the perspective of the Möbius loop, the question emerges for me as to whether mission has eclipsed formation. This mission focus seems to lack critical reflection on how persons within the conference are being formed by their most recent conflict. No public attempts at lament, reconciliation, or conflict transformation are evident. The most promising opportunity was the 2018 Celebration of Church Life, with the theme "Rebuild, Repair, Revive." But attention to formation at that event occurred through workshops presented in the context of teaching new believers—turning the focus again to outward mission and evangelism.[56]

While these are worthy gospel-centered goals, they are no substitute for the task of formation—in this case, internal healing and reconciliation within a broken faith community. As Osmer clarifies, "Formation is not something the congregation does to others, especially new members. It is something that must first happen to the congregation itself."[57] Moreover, in order to reach outward in mission, a faith community must nurture its own internal health; otherwise projection will thwart the community's best missional intentions.

We now turn to these considerations with the interpretive aids of missional theology and psychology.

Walking Worthily

As an Anabaptist practical theologian, I have had the honor and privilege of being mentored by missional theologian Darrell Guder, whose scholarship and practice inform mine. Guder identifies two parts to the church's engagement in God's mission: equipping and witnessing, like the two sides of our Möbius loop, formation and witness. Guder writes that gathered Christians "are equipped by God's Spirit to serve God as witnesses to the good news of God's healing purposes to the world."[58] In this equipping moment, the internal practices of the Christian community such as spiritual formation open the community to the possibility of God's transformation, forming it to "walk worthily" in light of its identity and calling.[59] Guder identifies the agent of formation as God's Spirit experienced in the Christian community's biblical engagement. This formation is a continual experience. He explains, "The calling of the missional community

56 Stella, "Lancaster Conference Begins New Era."

57 Osmer, "Formation in the Missional Church," 36.

58 Craig Ott, ed., *The Mission of the Church: Five Views in Conversation* (Grand Rapids, MI: Baker Academic, 2016), 22.

59 Darrell L. Guder, *Called to Witness: Doing Missional Theology*, The Gospel and Our Culture Series (Grand Rapids, MI: Eerdmans, 2015), 143.

is an ongoing process. . . . Precisely as walking, it is formed by the biblical imperatives that focus upon *how* the community walks, *how* its public conduct is to be congruent with its public testimony, and *how* it incarnates the good news that God wants all people to experience."[60] There are, thus, elements of internal formation and external witness in Guder's understanding of missional theology, and there is congruence between them.

Walking worthily, one of Guder's central concepts, comes from several of Paul's New Testament epistles that present the Christian imperative for walking through life in a manner that is a worthy representation of God and the call of the gospel.[61] Among many texts that refer to this worthy walking, Guder expounds on Philippians 1:27, the admonition to "live your life in a manner worthy of the gospel of Christ." Guder uses this passage to address how Christian communities walk in the world, living their lives in public and political dimensions. He explains, "It has to do with how their public conduct provides a credible demonstration of who Jesus Christ is and what his gospel now concretely means."[62] Undoubtedly, when a church's internal actions come into the public eye, as those of LMC's have, their lives are lived in public spaces.[63]

In addition to exploring the outward dimension of witness, as any missiologist would do, Guder also explores the inward dimension. Walking worthily has importance for the internal life of the church that may not explicitly be known outside the Christian community. Though Guder affirms the church's inner life as a form of outward witness, he doesn't merely collapse the two. He gives specific attention to how the inner life of the church is congruent with, but not reduced to or eclipsed by, its outward witness. Citing Jesus's linkage of identity, witness, and his disciples' visible love for one another (John 13:35), Guder levels a heavy charge against the internal character of the church community, naming divisiveness and division within the church as "totally unacceptable behaviors." He bluntly states, "Lovelessness within the community of faith is virtually a contradiction of the gospel. . . . An unreconciled community cannot really be a witness to the gospel of reconciliation. To do the witness to which we are called,

---

60 Guder, 135.

61 Guder, 129–30. These references include 1 Thess 2:10–12, 2 Thess 1:11, Col 1:9–10, and Eph 4:1–3.

62 Guder, 59–60.

63 For instance, the local Lancaster County newspaper picked up the story: Earle Cornelius, "Lancaster Mennonite Conference Leaves Mennonite Church USA Effective Monday," January 1, 2018, accessed November 4, 2019, https://lancasteronline.com/features/faith_values/lancaster-mennonite-conference-leaves-mennonite-church-usa-effective-monday/article_5cc14322-ecc9-11e7-b071-531e91668304.html.

then, the Christian community must learn to practice love as it is defined in the New Testament."[64]

What a word for Anabaptist communities that claim a peace theology! Practicing love does not mean ignoring differences but instead learning to "argue Christianly," as I have sometimes heard Guder put it. This allows the church to retain integrity in its witness.[65]

Guder makes it clear that a community's worthy walking does not assume a perfect community but rather a community dependent on God's grace. When those who follow Jesus fail, as his disciples certainly did, they are called to practice forgiveness and reconciliation.[66] Formation in the practices of dialogue, forgiveness, and reconciliation is therefore an important aspect of the church's identity. Indeed, Guder identifies reconciliation as the central theme of the gospel.[67] In Guder's edited volume *Missional Church: A Vision for the Sending of the Church in North America*, Inagrace Dietterich highlights reconciliation as a key ecclesial practice of missional communities. Entrusted with God's ministry of reconciliation (2 Cor 5:16–21), Christian communities are shaped by this ecclesial practice that includes confession, judgment, and forgiveness. Dietterich admits, "While central to the biblical understanding of the nature of salvation, reconciliation may be the most difficult practice for contemporary Christians even to consider, much less to actualize within their congregations."[68]

Like Guder, Dietterich calls for the demanding work of restoring community through reconciling dialogue, where differences and dissension are recognized and engaged in a constructive manner.[69] This is her vision for mutual accountability in Christian community, living the Christian way of life in a manner that is worthy of God's calling.[70] Guder puts it this way: "If the calling is to be agents of God's peace, then to live worthy of that calling is to live together peacefully as peacemakers. If the calling is to point to the healing that is God's intention for all creation, then to live worthy of that calling is to live together in ways that foster healing, restoration, and reconciliation."[71] This is

64 Darrell L. Guder, *Be My Witnesses: The Church's Mission, Message, and Messengers* (Grand Rapids, MI: Eerdmans, 1985), 125.

65 Guder, 128.

66 Guder, *Called to Witness*, 133.

67 Guder, *Be My Witnesses*, 80.

68 Inagrace Dietterich, "Missional Community: Cultivating Communities of the Holy Spirit," in *Missional Church: A Vision for the Sending of the Church in North America*, ed. Darrell L. Guder, The Gospel and Our Culture Series (Grand Rapids, MI: Eerdmans, 1998), 166.

69 Dietterich, 168.

70 Dietterich, 171.

71 Guder, *Called to Witness*, 117.

the vision for the church with integrity of witness, giving attention to both sides of the Möbius strip.

Mission as Projection?

When Christian communities experience conflict and division and do not seek to practice dialogue, forgiveness, healing, and reconciliation as Guder and Dietterich call for, they are in danger of operating out of the psychological phenomenon of projection. Among the many psychoanalysts who have studied this, C. G. Jung is the figure whose thought I will engage for this final aspect of analysis in this article. Jung calls negative aspects of the personality the shadow, and they initially exist on a subconscious level.[72] As long as this goes unengaged, the shadow will be projected onto other people. "Projections change the world into the replica of one's own unknown face," Jung suggests.[73]

Probably without intending to invoke psychology, Guder himself alludes to this unconscious process in his discussion of reductionism. He begins by naming the human inevitability of reducing the gospel as it is translated into human language and culture. This is not necessarily a problem; the negative aspect comes into play when control enters the scene and turns reduction into reductionism. "The danger rests in our desire to 'control God,'" Guder explains, "which leads us to regard our unavoidable reductions of the gospel as validated absolutes. We are constantly tempted to assert that our way of understanding the Christian faith is a final version of Christian truth."[74] Guder goes on to describe the historical trends of reductionisms throughout Christian history. He concludes, "The reductionisms of Western Christianity are very deeply rooted in a long history. They are, but now, largely unconscious."[75] I hear echoes of these kinds of unconscious theological absolutes in the calls I mentioned earlier within LMC for separation from cultural changes and persons with different ideas and commitments.

In Jungian analysis, the desire to control others is understood as a manifestation of unconscious, unintegrated, negative parts of the self that one seeks to bring under control in someone else. While we deny these aspects of ourselves, we seem to see them clearly in someone else.[76] Anabaptist pastoral theologian

---

72 Carl Gustav Jung, "Aion: The Phenomenology of the Self," in *The Portable Jung*, ed. Joseph Campbell, trans. R. F. C. Hull (New York: Viking, 1971), 145.

73 Jung, 146.

74 Darrell L. Guder, *The Continuing Conversion of the Church*, The Gospel and Our Culture Series (Grand Rapids, MI: Eerdmans, 2000), 100.

75 Guder, 102.

76 Ann Belford Ulanov and Alvin C. Dueck, *The Living God and Our Living Psyche: What Christians Can Learn from Carl Jung* (Grand Rapids, MI: Eerdmans, 2008), 16.

David Augsburger explains what happens within groups that possess a collective shadow. He writes, "As the shadow emerges, the group's identity becomes sharply defined, its beliefs more rigid, its convictions more passionate."[77] The longer this goes on, the more extreme the projection gets. The community's "perspectives become compulsively dogmatic, unwittingly arrogant, unadmittedly dictatorial, and increasingly intolerant of diversity or challenge."[78] I see some evidence of these behaviors in the LMC situation. Those negative unconscious aspects that are embedded in the faith community become projected onto neighbors, both within and beyond the church.[79]

A shifted focus on mission brings an array of new neighbors into the reach of a community living with unresolved conflicts. This creates the conditions for additional harm. In his book on church planting, Stuart Murray warns, "If church planting is an attempt to avert attention from unresolved issues, it can cause serious relational and institutional damage," which, if left unaddressed, "will over time become damaging, inhibiting, and destructive."[80] If this is the case, how can a community that has been formed in the crucible of internal conflict bear witness with integrity to the gospel of reconciliation?

The Möbius Vision

While formation is, in part, a human-driven phenomenon, it is also the locus of divine action. Christians are formed both by human community and by God's Spirit. In the Anabaptist context, we could say that formation is the Holy Spirit's shaping of persons into the form of Christ (Phil 2:1–11). Menno Simons identifies this formation as regeneration, an act "of God, through the living Word," so that believers can have the nature, mind, disposition, and "aptitude for good" that Christ demonstrated in his human form.[81] This formation enacted by God is the regeneration of God's image in the believer.[82]

Undoubtedly, human beings play an important role in formation. Jungian scholar Ann Bedford Ulanov invites us to name and face the negative aspects

---

77 David W. Augsburger, *Hate-Work: Working through the Pain and Pleasures of Hate* (Louisville, KY: Westminster John Knox, 2004), 103.

78 Augsburger, 103.

79 Jung, "Aion: The Phenomenology of the Self," 53.

80 Stuart Murray, *Planting Churches in the 21st Century: A Guide for Those Who Want Fresh Perspectives and New Ideas for Creating Congregations* (Scottdale, PA: Herald, 2010), 48–49.

81 Menno Simons, "The Spiritual Resurrection, c. 1536," in *The Complete Writings of Menno Simons, c.1496–1561*, ed. J. C. Wenger, trans. Leonard Verduin (Scottdale, PA: Herald, 1956), 55.

82 Simons, 56.

of ourselves and our communities, and consciously struggle with those aspects until we experience transformation. This is work we can engage in even as we await the transformation enacted by God's Spirit. If human conflict can form us in particular ways, so can human attempts at forgiveness and reconciliation, empowered and led by God's Spirit. This hard work means facing what we wish was not true about ourselves, accepting its existence, and then, as Ulanov says, "to come face to face with the astounding fact that Paul announces: God loves us while we are yet sinners."[83] Indeed, this brings us to Guder's claim that "the first form of incarnational witness of the church is constant testimony to its forgiveness, and its need for continuing forgiveness."[84] Embracing God's love of ourselves as forgiven sinners enables us to witness to the gospel of reconciliation in our very being.

Returning to the Möbius Loop as Continuous Formation-Witness

In this article, I have described several models of Anabaptist witness, engaged an extended example of formation and witness in LMC, cited Guder's call to walk worthily, and tapped into the psychological concept of projection. In sum, the Möbius twist I am proposing for Anabaptist witness is the retention of both formation and witness in the life of the church. Each is distinct, essential, and should not be collapsed into the other. The integrity of Anabaptist witness depends on its attention to and congruency with formation.

Even when we engage the formational task of reconciliation in the wake of church conflict, as I hope LMC will do, we do not have to put witness on hold. Jesus, after all, doesn't wait until his followers are perfectly formed to send them out to bear witness to the good news and heal the sick. We see throughout the Gospels this constant movement back and forth between when Jesus spends time forming his disciples and when they engage in witness. Jesus continues to tend to their spiritual practices, teaching, and treatment of one another. Formation and witness continue simultaneously in the disciples' experience, like the continuous motion of the Möbius loop. May it be so among Anabaptist communities.

---

83 Ulanov and Dueck, *The Living God and Our Living Psyche*, 54–55.

84 Guder, *Be My Witnesses*, 31.

Anabaptist Hermeneutical Formation and Witness in Meserete Kristos Church of Ethiopia

Endaweke Tsegaw

For centuries, the central hallmark of Anabaptist conviction has been a shared identity as successor of the Apostolic church—a church that refused infant baptism, mystical change of the Lord's Supper, and military service. To this list, Frits Kuiper adds biblicism and congregational hermeneutics of Anabaptist interpretation of Scripture.[1] As a congregation in which the Master and disciples unite through adult baptism, the Anabaptist church viewed unconscious baptism as tantamount to blasphemy.[2] In this context, the church as the true ekklesia separated from the state, choosing to belong instead to the Kingdom of God that both is and is to come.[3]

Stuart Murray further summarizes Anabaptist hermeneutical convictions into the following six main principles: Scripture as self-interpreting, Christo-centrism, the complementarity of two testaments, the consistency of the Spirit and the Word, congregational hermeneutics, and the hermeneutics of obedi-

Endaweke Tsegaw (LLB, LLM, and Assistant professor of law) has been teaching, researching, and engaging in community service in Dire-Dawa (Ethiopia) University and the surrounding area for more than fifteen years. He has also served as Dean of the College of Law and Director of Legal Affairs at the university. His research and publication areas are human rights and access to justice and peace. In addition, he serves the Dire Dawa MKC in various departments. He is pursuing an MA in Theology and Global Anabaptism (Ethiopia Cohort) at AMBS.

1 Frits Kuiper, "The Pre-Eminence of the Bible in Mennonite History," in Essays on Biblical Interpretation: Anabaptist-Mennonite Perspectives, Occasional Papers, no. 1, ed. Willard M. Swartley (Elkhart, IN: Institute of Mennonite Studies, 1984), 117–28.

2 Kuiper, "The Pre-Eminence of the Bible," 118.

3 Kuiper, "The Pre-Eminence of the Bible," 120.

ence.[4] John D. Roth recommends that Anabaptists also enhance their convictions about discipleship, worship and praise, and loving to live between times.5 Modern and postmodern Anabaptist interpretations, drawing from feminist and liberation theologies, add that Anabaptist formation should include politically disadvantaged community groups not addressed by creeds of early Anabaptists.[6] And fundamentalist theologians, on the other hand, in contrast to the early Anabaptists, bring a quest for justification of war and slavery.[7]

Although Anabaptism's formation practices have clearly diversified through the ages, its founding theologies and traditions continue to influence followers of the Reformers and other Christian groups, the largest of which is the Ethiopian Mennonite church, Meserete Kristos Church (MKC). This article explores how some key convictions of biblical interpretation by past and present Anabaptists have influenced the formation and witness of MKC.

Anabaptism through the Ages

This section summarizes early, modern, and postmodern Anabaptist interpretive approaches and how those approaches have given shape to the formation and witness of MKC as evidenced in MKC's core interpretive convictions.

Early Anabaptism

Anabaptism was born out of a Bible study circle in the Zurich reformation led by Ulrich Zwingli in the sixteenth century.[8] It was then instituted by radicals whose conviction about adult baptism rippled out far beyond Zwingli.[9] Although the Anabaptist-Mennonite movement was composed of a group of laymen, all members were considered ministers (priests and prophets).[10] Discon-

---

4 Stuart Murray, *Biblical Interpretation in the Anabaptist Tradition*, Studies in the Believers Church Tradition, no. 2 (Kitchener, ON: Pandora, 2000), 31.

5 John D. Roth, *Living Between the Times: "The Anabaptist Vision and Mennonite Reality" Revisited*, accessed April 6, 2022, https://www.goshen.edu/mhl/Refocusing/JOHNRROTH.HTM.

6 Willard M. Swartley, *Slavery, Sabbath, War, and Women: Case Issues in Biblical Interpretation* (Scottdale, PA: Herald, 1983), 22.

7 Swartley, *Slavery, Sabbath, War, and Women*, 22.

8 William R. Estep, *The Anabaptist Story* (Nashville, TN: Broadman, 1963), 10. The fathers of Swiss Anabaptism, such as Conrad Grebel, Felix Manz, George Blaurock, and Simon Stumpf, were drawn into Zwingli's Greek class but eventually deviated from his teachings after serious disagreement regarding infant baptism; mass and images of the church; and separation of state and church.

9 Estep, *The Anabaptist Story*, 10.

10 Kuiper, "Pre-eminence of the Bible," 128.

tent over the practices of the Catholic Church and Reformers, whose hierarchal ecclesiastical interpretation of the Bible facilitated rampant individual celebrity among church ministers,[11] Anabaptists encouraged ordinary individuals in the congregation to interpret Scripture. This move to interpretation by the common person has also been attributed to the fact that ordinary persons could not access the corpus of Scripture.[12] Anabaptists also rejected the Reformers' doctrinal commitments and fixed convictions, which had been sought from political authorities and the state church.[13] Accordingly, the borders of formation in Anabaptist hermeneutics through the ages have often been drawn by Protestant churches.

Early Anabaptists believed that Scripture was best understood in a congregation.[14] A typical example of interpretation is portrayed in this statement by Swiss Anabaptists: "When brothers and sisters are together, they shall take up something to read together. The one to whom God has given the best understanding shall explain it; the others should be still and listen."[15] On the more extreme end of this sentiment, some Anabaptist writers preferred that the leader oversee a smooth communal hermeneutic process as a facilitator only, not also as a participant.[16] Biblicism that presupposes the singular authority of Scripture as a transparent, luminous, and simple revelation of the will of God seemed clear to them. They believed that the Bible is sufficient in and of itself to be understood.[17]

Early Anabaptists also linked their biblical interpretation with discipleship and obedience. Ethical obedience to Scripture influenced how they interpreted the Bible; they trusted that personal obedience to the standard of Christ's lifestyle would guard against subjectivity of application. Critics of this understanding pointed out that, conversely, there is no correlation between interpretation and obedience.[18] While Reformers gave precedence to theology over obedience,[19] Anabaptists contended that obedience leads to suffering,

---

11 Murray, *Biblical Interpretation*, 157.

12 Walter Klaassen, "Anabaptist Hermeneutics: Presuppositions, Principles and Practice" in *Essays on Biblical Interpretation: Anabaptist-Mennonite Perspectives*, Occasional Papers, no. 1, ed. Willard Swartley (Elkhart, IN: Institute of Mennonite Studies, 1984), 10.

13 Murray, *Biblical Interpretation*, 159.

14 Klassen, "Anabaptist Hermeneutics," 9.

15 Murray, *Biblical Interpretation*, 161.

16 Murray, *Biblical Interpretation*, 163,164.

17 Murray, *Biblical Interpretation*, 38.

18 Murray, *Biblical Interpretation*, 189.

19 Murray, *Biblical Interpretation*, 188.

which maximizes the potential to explore the life of Christ in the Scripture and to live like him.[20] For Anabaptists, preaching the gospel or doing mission was also central to obedience, whereas Reformers' focus on church institutions and territory lacked integrity with a pastoral approach.[21] The more that early Anabaptists approached Scripture diligently with faith, the more they believed they would better understand the Scripture through the Holy Spirit, the highest interpreter to illuminate the Word.[22] Without this proper understanding of Scripture, activism and superficial application of textual interpretation, in their view, would be harmful.

Modern and Postmodern Anabaptism

Modern and postmodern Anabaptists have developed newer traditions that supplant early Anabaptist scriptural interpretation formulations, including the use of historical criticism, liberation theology, feminist theology, and theology of war and slavery.[23] The historical critical method preserves the integrity and authority of the Bible by providing a remedy for the apparent contradiction of the texts and avoiding interpreter bias, based on the conviction that what God communicates is errorless and consistent throughout times and contexts. Consider, for instance, the following texts dealing with slavery and war that seem inconsistent across the Bible:[24] slavery under Moses (Lev 19:18, 25:44–46) and slavery in Paul's time (1 Tim 6:1–6) both seem to contradict Jesus's teaching to "love your neighbor as yourself."[25] These apparent contradictions, which have led to debate against and for slavery and war by many Western theologians, are abridged and resolved by the historical critical method, which enables the interpreter to "submit his/her own prejudices, tradition, and pre-established beliefs to a fresh encounter with Scripture as divine Word."[26] Utilizing but moving beyond the historical critical method, Willard Swartley calls for a holistic approach to Scripture that explores three interacting worlds of biblical

20 Murray, *Biblical Interpretation*, 197.

21 Murray, *Biblical Interpretation*, 201.

22 Murray, *Biblical Interpretation*, 187.

23 These more recent ways of approaching the biblical text are not evenly accepted by MKC local congregations.

24 Swartley, *Slavery, Sabbath, War, Women*, 117, 143.

25 Swartley, *Slavery, Sabbath, War, Women*, 48.

26 Willard M Swartley, "Beyond the Historical-Critical Method," in *Essays on Biblical Interpretation: Anabaptist-Mennonite Perspectives*, Occasional Papers, no. 1, ed. Willard M. Swartley (Elkhart, IN: Institute of Mennonite Studies, 1984), 246.

interpretation: the world behind the text, the world within the text, and the world in front of the text.[27]

Some Anabaptists go even further. While John Howard Yoder's *The Politics of Jesus* sought to reaffirm most of the convictions of early Anabaptists,[28] his critics offered *Liberating the Politics of Jesus*,[29] which argues for the inclusion of politically marginalized groups into Anabaptism. As Western political philosophy centered and propagated democracy, rule of law, and human rights after 1945 (WWII), simultaneously liberation and feminist theologies ushered in these politics based on the conviction that interpretation of the Scripture should adopt social change. While there are constructive feminist approaches, Lydia Harder notes that there are also negative approaches that are suspicious of any form of interpretation of experiences from persons outside the feminist communities.[30]

Some Anabaptist interpreters view Christological convictions as coopted by a culture of racism, violence, and dehumanization.[31] Accordingly, the proponents of liberation theology argue that the heart of the gospel proclamation of salvation includes liberation of politically oppressed people.[32] Some call for Anabaptist-Mennonites to also include a cultural model of disability.[33] While this perspective is crucial, it is important to recognize that some liberationist views focus so intently on the oppressive function of the biblical texts that they fail to see the possibility that these texts could have more than one legitimate interpretation.[34]

---

27 Willard M. Swartley, "Peace and Violence in the New Testament," in eds. Laura L. Brenneman and Brad D. Schantz, *Struggles for Shalom: Peace and Violence Across the Testaments*, Studies in Peace and Scripture, vol. 12 (Eugene, OR: Pickwick, 2014), 152.

28 John Howard Yoder, *The Politics of Jesus: Vicit Agnus Noster*, 2nd ed. (Carlisle, UK: Paternoster, 1994), 87.

29 Elizabeth Soto Albrecht and Daryl W. Stephens, *Liberating the Politics of Jesus: Renewing Peace Theology through the Wisdom of Women* (New York, T & T Clark, 2020).

30 Lydia Neufeld Harder, "Obedience, Suspicion, and the Gospel of Mark: A Mennonite-Feminist Exploration of Biblical Authority," *Studies in Women and Religion*, vol. 5 (Waterloo, ON: Wilfrid Laurier University Press, 1998), 95.

31 Elizabeth Soto Albrecht and Darryl W. Stephens, *Liberating the Politics of Jesus: Renewing Peace Theology through the Wisdom of Women*. (New York: T&T Clark, 2020), 18.

32 Albrecht and Stephens, *Liberating the Politics of Jesus*, 60.

33 Melanie A. Howard, "Jesus' Healing Ministry in New Perspective: Towards a Cultural Model of Disability in Anabaptist-Mennonite Hermeneutics," *The Conrad Grebel Review* 38, no. 2 (2020), accessed April 7, 2022, https://uwaterloo.ca/grebel/publications/conrad-grebel-review/issues/spring-2020/jesus-healing-ministry-new-perspective-towards-cultural.

34 Harder, *Obedience, Suspicion, and the Gospel of Mark*, 94.

Anabaptist Formation and Witness in Meserete Kristos Church (MKC)

Echoes of Anabaptism's early core convictions and their formational and scriptural interpretative traditions can be heard in various regions of the world. One of those places is Ethiopia, where people found a resonance with Anabaptist formational practices that they had not experienced with other religions of the country in the 1940s and 1950s. This resulted in the birth of Meserete Kristos Church (MKC). In the years since, MKC has adopted from modern and postmodern Anabaptists the following six formational practices: (1) congregational hermeneutics, (2) Christocentrism, (3) nonviolent resistance, (4) separation of church and state, (5) women's inclusion in ministry, and (6) historical critical methods of biblical interpretation. But first, a brief history of MKC's beginnings.

The Birth of MKC

The mission and witness of the Kingdom of God using the distinctive theology of the Anabaptist tradition started in Nazareth (Adama) in 1946 in response to the aftermath of WWII by the Mennonite Relief Committee (MRC) from Elkhart, Indiana.[35] In 1948 the Eastern Mennonite Board of Missions and Charities (EMBMC) took over the work and established the Mennonite Mission in Ethiopia. Daniel and Blanche Sensenig were the first mission director couple. As a result of an agreement with Emperor Haile Selassie, the Mennonites could evangelize among the Muslims and pagans but not the Orthodox, because Nazareth was an "Orthodox area."[36] This effectively meant that the missionaries were not allowed to preach outside their compound, since the Emperor's closed policy encompassed the northern and central part of the country.[37]

In Nazareth, Mennonites transformed the Italian cotton-gaining mill into the Haile Mariam Mamo Hospital (now Adama Referral Hospital), where they started the Dresser Bible School for nurse aides. There they taught Bible along with medical subjects to Orthodox young people.[38] As a result, on June 16, 1951, a secret baptism was arranged in Addis Ababa at a missionary home in Gulele. On this memorable Saturday, ten people were baptized and Meserete Kristos Church was born.[39]

35 Tilahun Beyene, *I Will Build My Church* (Addis Ababa: Mega Printing Enterprises, 2002), 28. Translation of the Amharic texts of the Book to English is mine.

36 Beyene, *I Will Build My Church*, 28.

37 Beyene, *I Will Build My Church*, 34.

38 Beyene, *I Will Build My Church*, 34.

39 Beyene, *I Will Build My Church*, 69.

In many ways, the birth of MKC resembles the birth of Anabaptism itself: The numbers of people and the secret scene of its beginnings—hidden away from infant baptizers and the state—were the same.[40] And the name of the church—Meserete Kristos/foundation of Christ—was inspired by 1 Corinthians 3:11, which was the banner Scripture of early Anabaptist Mennonites and the foundation for the arguments of their leader, Menno Simons.

Naming the new church proved to be a challenging task for both the foreign missionaries and the Ethiopian leaders because each group was competing to have their own interests represented in the name. Many options were placed on the table:[41] the missionaries expressed their firm desire to include the name "Anabaptist" or "Mennonite" or both, while the Ethiopians resisted abandoning their tutor (Anabaptist Mennonite) and came up with the name "Meserete Kristos." Six alternative names were presented for discussion: Meserete Kristos Association, Meserete Kristos (Mennonite) Association, Meserete Kristos Mennonite Association, Meserete Kristos Church, Meserete Kristos (Mennonite) Church, and Meserete Kristos Mennonite Church. After a long debate over these options, on August 16, 1956, the group finally came to consensus on the name "Meserete Kristos Church."

By 2020, almost seventy years after the first baptism, MKC had grown to more than 1,140 local congregations with more than 650,000 members. While the congregations have engaged in various faith practices, the core convictions of Anabaptism are protected in bylaws, teachings, leadership styles, and training by the MKC seminaries.

Six Formational Anabaptist Practices in MKC

1. Congregational Hermeneutics and Bible Study

Like the early Anabaptists, who resisted contemporary challenges from Catholics and Reformers, MKC responded to Ethiopia's prosecution of communism by holding underground Bible studies and then living out their congregational interpretation of Anabaptism.[42] By the very nature of the Bible study circle, the members and leaders were not identified by name but instead were all known as "brothers" and "sisters," thereby protecting them from

40 The missionaries were forced to work in secret in Eastern Ethiopia in Harar province at Deder and Bedeno.

41 Beyene, *I Will Build My Church*, 81.

42 Kelbessa Muleta Demena and Mary H. Schertz, "The Text Has Something to Tell Us! Bible Teaching in the Meserete Kristos Church, Ethiopia," *Vision: A Journal for Church and Theology* 11, no. 2 (Fall 2010): 78–86.

insurgents knowing and using their names for prosecution.[43] In addition, the location of the Bible study would sometimes change from week to week for the same purpose. This ended up actually aiding evangelism and mission as the number of believers increased at a very fast rate.

In general, Bible study in MKC today remains as it was in the days of the early Anabaptists—an assembly of lay persons who participate in interpreting the text according to their own understandings. And the leader's role is limited to facilitating all the members' engagement in the study. The meetings serve as a forum that creates a social bond among members and also identifies people who need help. In spite of the nonparticipation of many members of the church, Bible study remains the central formational practice of MKC in Ethiopia.[44]

2. Christocentrism

The early Anabaptists were very intentional about training new believers. That training included teaching the faith statements of Hubmaier's Catechism of 1526 and the Schleitheim Confession of 1527. These statements are now replicated in the "Shared Convictions of Global Anabaptists of 2006."[45]

Christocentrism is another hallmark early-Anabaptist practice embraced by MKC. It is reflected in the church's faith statement book, the teaching books of disciples and sermons, and congregational decisions. One example of MKC's adoption of Christocentrism is found in the church's book for teaching disciples entitled *Following Christ*, which focuses on how believers can practice and imitate the teachings and the life of Christ. This material was recently revised and has been used by many evangelical and Baptist denominations in Ethiopia.[46]

Another example of Christocentric practice can be seen in the discernment by MKC's 2017 General Assembly that thirteen persons—who were so-called prophets, apostles, bishops, and pastors in Ethiopia and a diaspora abroad—should be classified as heretics, false prophets, and false teachers because their teachings and practices were identified as contrary to the supremacy of Christ. By virtue of this decision, these persons were not allowed to preach or teach in the pulpits of MKC, and MKC members could not participate in their congregation. Politically empowered persons who ridiculed the Assembly's decision called for police arrest of the MKC president. A counter movement of

---

43 Demena and Shertz, "The Text Has Something to Tell Us!," 78–86.

44 Demena and Shertz, "The Text Has Something to Tell Us!."

45 C. Arnold Snyder, *Anabaptist History and Theology* (Scottdale, PA: Pandora, 2002), 83.

46 MKC is one of only a few church groups in Ethiopia that have their own teaching materials for disciples.

MKC members, however, managed to secure a prompt acquittal of the charges, and the arrest lasted no longer than three hours.

Stigmatization of the church went on for some time. Although the mainline Protestant churches followed the decision of MKC, it was not welcomed by all members of the church. For instance, I was internally challenged to read before the congregation the circular letter containing the decision issued by the head office of MKC, because two of the persons involved in the controversy had previously served in conference programs in my local church. Specifically, I had brought one of them from abroad who served in a teaching conference a year before the decision. Through my studies at Anabaptist Mennonite Biblical Seminary, I realized the decision had been influenced by Anabaptist Christocentric theology.

Moreover, the same Assembly of the church took a stand to not ordain its ministers as prophets and apostles. The Theological Commission of the Church proposed to the General Assembly that the titles "prophet" and "apostle" had been abused by people clinging to false practices and false teachings and that using such titles would be contrary to the church's tradition of Christocentrism. As a result, the Assembly stated that since God's grace is given to the church, the gift of the Holy Spirit should be free to work without ordination. This decision was not endorsed by many servants.

3. Nonviolent Resistance

MKC has teaching material dealing with "conflict resolution" for its leaders and servants, and the head of MKC is involved with social peace work in collaboration with the concerned branch of government. This work includes training on subjects of peace for selected non-believer university and high school students in different regions of the country. It also includes engaging in settlement of ethnic conflicts in the country.

Ethiopia is a conflict-ridden country, however, with war currently breaking out in the northern region, and most believers share the overriding sentiment of resisting or supporting war against the "other." There is not much room for messages of nonviolent resistance in the pulpits of Protestant churches in general and MKC in particular. Purposeful preaching and teaching of Jesus's Sermon on the Mount, specifically Matthew 5:38, is getting old, and believers are largely being left to manage their own personal responses to war.

4. Church and State

In relation to the state, MKC teaches its members that they are not to participate in politics but are allowed to engage in peace and development activities of the community. Particularly, leaders of the church should not be members of political parties, in order to stay true to the conviction that the interests of the two kingdoms—the Kingdom of God and the kingdom of the world—contradict each other.

This teaching creates a problem, however, in the rural churches, where every public servant is expected to be a member of the ruling party. If these churches were to follow this guideline, they would have no believers who could serve as leaders. Thus, for rural areas MKC has developed an exception that allows members of a political party to assume leadership roles in the church.

An additional complicating factor regarding MKC's relationship to the state is that the political landscape of Ethiopia is currently changing in many sectors. For instance, because the incumbent prime minister, along with many ministers and higher officials, are evangelical Protestant, MKC members and leaders have been influenced to support political involvement. By doing so, MKC is compromising its conviction that state and church should be separate.

5. Women as Leaders in the Church

The inclusion of women as ministers of the church is also a new spiritual phenomenon within MKC as a result of modern and postmodernism influences. Two decades ago women were barred from ministerial positions, but that practice has recently changed, and women pastors are now allowed to serve the church. Leading spiritual ceremonies like marriage, communion, funerals, and so on, however, is still not permitted for women; these remain as patriarchal services within MKC.

6. Historical Critical Biblical Interpretation

MKC applies a historical critical method of interpretation mostly in its theological seminaries and teaching sermons. The method helps to explore which historical events matter for the text—ascertaining the time period, the first audience, and other possible contexts in which the Scripture was developed. The MKC Bible study guide material uses an inductive system in which observations, interpretation, and implementation of the texts are incorporated. In sermons, teaching and preaching based on a historical critical method has become more accepted than other methods.

With the proliferation of charismatic movements in most places, however, allegorical interpretation and "spirit-led ministries" or psychology-led ministries are engulfing the MKC. Moreover, the introduction of the appointment of "Senior Pastor" in local churches—which brings with the title spiritual and administrative mandates in addition to committee leadership—has caused some deviation from congregational interpretation as a foundational practice of MKC members.

Embracing Anabaptist Hermeneutics and Practice for Effective Witness

Anabaptism offers noble formation practices that help the church live out a Christ-like life now and in preparation for the Kingdom to come. In today's world of spiritual fluidity where celebrity of preachers with their heretical traditions is common, MKC has chosen instead to embrace the early Anabaptist interpretative traditions: congregational hermeneutics with Scripture as self-interpreting; Christocentrism with the complementarity of two testaments and a hermeneutics of obedience; and nonviolent resistance. MKC has also responded positively to the separation of church and state; modern and postmodern Anabaptists' inclusion of women and colored persons; and historical criticism methods of interpretation.

Accordingly, these legacies of Anabaptism are highly reflected in the Meserete Kristos Church of Ethiopia and MKC seminaries. As MKC teaches its Anabaptist identity intentionally, it will prepare its members for the Kingdom of God now and in the future. I appeal to other Anabaptist Mennonite churches in the world to likewise form their members in Anabaptist hermeneutics and practices, thus preparing all for effective witness.

Formed as (Sexual) Peacemakers?

Interrogating the Role of Sexuality in Relation to Institutional Culture for Formation for Witness and Discipleship at Postsecondary Theological Schools

Kimberly Penner

Danielle is a queer Mennonite undergraduate student studying theology and living in residence at a Mennonite university. She is excited to live away from home for the first time. She is excited to make new friends and to date new people. The residence code of conduct assumes a gender binary (men and women) and states that men and women must live in separate residences (presumably to prevent premarital heterosexual sex). Sex is stated as being for marriage. Sex is not defined, and sexuality more broadly understood is not mentioned. Rather than enforce the residence rules, the approach of the Residence Assistants or "Dons" at Danielle's residence is "Don't ask, don't tell." Both approaches raise a lot of questions for Danielle. She wonders how faith and sexuality relate, if they relate, for her. Even though the university claims to celebrate diversity, she reads between the lines of the residence policy and feels like who she is as a sexual person is not openly celebrated. She wonders if there is another path besides what she gleans from the university residence rules and the lack of any clear ethic from the culture in her residence. Are there any possibilities for bringing together her faith and sexuality in life-giving, liberating ways? She wishes she had more support to figure out the answer to that question.

Nate enrolls in an academic program at a theological school to earn a degree that will educate and form him for congregational witness and service as a minister. He takes the required courses in theology, Bible, spiritual care, worship, and ethics. He learns about power and privilege, the importance of maintaining healthy sexual boundaries in ministry, and the importance of professional ethics more broadly. He does well. He gets good grades, and his peers appreciate him and his comments in class. Nate grew up steeped in purity culture.[1] As he

Kimberly Penner works both as a full-time pastor at Stirling Avenue Mennonite Church in Kitchener, Ontario, Canada, and an adjunct instructor. She has taught Christian ethics at Conrad Grebel University College (Waterloo, Ontario) and ethics at Victoria College in the University of Toronto. She especially enjoys talking about power, peace, violence, embodiment, and sexuality in the life of the church and beyond.

reflects on his faith journey, he shares with his peers that this upbringing made him associate sexual desire and sexual acts before marriage as sinful and that this perpetuated a great deal of shame for him about his own sexual desires. He longs for a life-giving sexual ethic that affirms him as a sexual person, especially as he continues to struggle with feelings of shame, self-loathing, and sexual fantasies involving violence. He keeps these struggles to himself, feeling too sinful to talk about them with others. Nate graduates from the program and goes on to become a pastor. Years later, news comes out that he has sexually assaulted a youth in the congregation. As faculty and students meet to process this news, they wonder what more could be done to prevent this from happening in the future.

These stories raise questions about how and where formation happens on the campuses of theological schools, institutional responsibility to form students who do no harm, and the relationship between sexuality and faith formation for students. I claim that the contextual nature of theological education is sexually situated and, therefore, that sexuality matters for formation for witness and discipleship.[2] If Anabaptist-Mennonite postsecondary institutions—particularly their theological programs—seek to form students for witness and discipleship that embodies the values of peace and justice, then we as people in these institutions must pay attention to our religious narratives and institutional culture[3] around sexuality; we must identify elements that produce discriminatory and abusive outcomes and promote those that are liberating and life-giving.

I begin with the contextual and political nature of theological education. Engaging the work of Willie James Jennings in *After Whiteness: An Education in Belonging*, I agree that theological formation is shaped by its Western, patriarchal, colonial history. I elaborate that this history is also a history of sexuality—for example, of theological and ethical understandings of sexuality, of sexualized and racialized others, and of sexuality as a patriarchal and colonial tool to control subjugated peoples. I then draw on Sarah Ahmed's work to fur-

1 Purity culture in evangelicalism promotes abstinence, heterosexuality, and an understanding of gender as a binary (male and female), with men needing to be the strong leaders of the household and women needing to be supportive mothers and wives. Purity culture "is centered on the belief that girls' and women's social 'value' is contingent on their virginity/chastity and their ability to remain sexually 'pure.' Rooted in patriarchal gender ideals, it fetishizes virginity" (Caroline Blyth, *Rape Culture, Purity Culture, and Coercive Control in Teen Girl Bibles* [London, Routledge, 2021], 10).

2 I also believe the same is true for Western education more broadly, but for the sake of this article I will limit myself to arguments about theological education.

3 When I speak of institutional culture in this paper, I am including normative actions, signs, symbols, categories, and knowledge through which a community performs its identity and is, therefore, defined.

ther reveal how this history continues to negatively shape experiences in the academy today via cultures of sexual abuse and harassment. Ahmed's work also illustrates the importance of looking to complaints about abuses of power as important sources for institutional ethics. To make the connection to formation, I demonstrate how institutional culture, not only course content and pedagogy, is influential for student formation for sexual peace and justice, citing research by Marilyn Naidoo. Finally, I offer suggestions for how to form students for witness and discipleship as sexual beings committed to peace and justice.

Formation is Sexually Situated

Anabaptist-Mennonite postsecondary institutions do not guarantee formation, nor do they license students for ministry. Yet formation, most often cited as formation for ministry, remains a common goal: formation for "service to church and society" as someone who "engage[s] issues of justice and peace and attend[s] to voices of the marginalized,"[4] formation for "service to others, peacemaking, cross-cultural engagement and sustainability,"[5] faith formation for "the good of the mission and health of the church."[6] Somehow, theological education and life at a theological school is not only about learning new information and academic skills but also, ideally, about forming students to live out the values of the institution, informed by the values of the gospel. Theological formation is about the "ongoing development of identity, reclaiming one's culture, gender and other aspects of identity; it is part of moving towards greater authenticity."[7]

As a sessional instructor who teaches Christian ethics at a Mennonite institution, I am filled with excitement and hope at the possibility of mutual formation for peace and justice. It gives added meaning and purpose to the work we do in the classroom and the kind of positive impact we can have on the church and society. Willie James Jennings, Associate Professor of Systematic Theology and Africana Studies at Yale Divinity School and former Dean of Academic Programs at Duke University Divinity School, says it well when he writes:

> Education and theological education kill the lie that people don't change. Formation happens, people do change, even if that change is not easily perceived by impatient eyes. I have seen many kinds of formation, many befores

4 "Theological Studies," Conrad Grebel University College, accessed February 27, 2022, https://uwaterloo.ca/theological-studies/about#mission.

5 "About EMU," Eastern Mennonite University, accessed February 27, 2022, https://emu.edu/about/.

6 "Graduate School of Theology and Ministry," Canadian Mennonite University, accessed February 27, 2022, https://www.cmu.ca/academics/gstm.

7 Marilyn Naidoo, "An Ethnographic Study on Managing Diversity in Two Protestant Theological Colleges," *HTS Theological Studies* 72, no. 1 (2016): 1–7, 2.

> and many afters, among undergraduates, graduate students, and doctoral students. Even newly minted scholars becoming new faculty members and moving from the early years of teaching to the mature years to the senior season participate in a formation process.[8]

The possibility of formation for witness and discipleship that is committed to peace and justice as we learn and grow together is exciting. That said, and as Jennings argues, the formation that takes place in theological education, and Western education in general, is also troubled and distorted.[9]

I agree with Jennings that as much as formation can reflect change and character development for the better, we also need to wrestle with the fact that theological education has been and continues to be a distorted formation. Jennings spends much of *After Whiteness* explaining this distortion—a formation of the student into the image of a "white self-sufficient man, his self-sufficiency defined by possession, control, and mastery"[10] and its connection to the crisis of decline in theological education. In short, he claims it is formed between two things: "a pedagogical imagination calibrated to forming white self-sufficient men and a related pedagogical imagination calibrated to forming a Christian racial and cultural homogeneity that yet performs the nationalist vision of that same white self-sufficient man."[11] While this is a problem that affects all of Western education, Jennings argues that it was born of theological education itself.[12]

In the history of Christianity and its missions, the spread of the gospel goes hand in hand with colonialism. For, as Jennings states, while translation of the gospel opened endless possibilities of boundary-crossing freedom and life, it also opened the possibilities of boundary-crossing slavery and death.[13] The teacher and the translator have the power to "call worlds into existence through words spoken and written."[14] Sadly, teachers and translators often called into existence worlds of domination and subordination, of the White savior and the sinful, dark-skinned Other in need of saving, who was also to be exploited, conquered, and enslaved.[15]

---

8 Willie James Jennings, *After Whiteness: An Education in Belonging* (Grand Rapids, MI: William B. Eerdmans, 2020), x.

9 Jennings, x.

10 Jennings, xi.

11 Jennings, xi,

12 Jennings, xi

13 Jennings, xii.

14 Jennings, xii.

15 See Kelly Brown Douglas's work on the racial and sexual stereotypes of Black people by White culture and White Christianity as a tool of both slavery and Christian

This history still reveals itself in theological education and continues to negatively impact students today. As I look back at my own experience as a doctoral student at a consortium of theological schools, I now recognize the ways in which I too was being formed into the image of the White, self-sufficient male. Even though I was critical of this image as a feminist theo-ethicist, I felt the anxiety of needing to conform to it to succeed. I was trying to publish more and be smarter by knowing more, to dispense that same knowledge to others and prop myself up. I felt the temptation to view my classmates as competition. To an extent, which I was largely unconscious of, I adopted the myth of meritocracy (that I would get what I wanted by simply working harder and that I would deserve whatever I accomplished, more so than others who did not achieve what I did).

Self-sufficiency was implicitly understood, and sometimes explicitly stated, as the goal of our education. At the same time that I claimed I valued my physical, emotional, and spiritual well-being as a student, I also sacrificed my health and well-being to keep up academically. Even with a doctoral supervisor who promoted and embodied feminist values—who emphasized collaboration over competition, offered affirmations alongside critique, bought me lunch and tried to incorporate yoga breaks into our class time—the distorted goal of formation remained powerful. There was enough of the distorted image of the self-sufficient White male in my coursework, perpetuated by some of my male classmates and promoted by the history and hierarchy of academia, that I found myself feeling depressed and anxious about succeeding. It was especially overwhelming as a pregnant woman having a child during my PhD studies and not wanting to fall behind, not to mention the need to find part-time employment to help support myself and my partner financially. Ultimately, I was still dependent on conforming to academy to succeed as an academic, which meant becoming some version of the self-sufficient White male.

The history of theological education in the West is also a history of sexuality. Although Jennings spends less time on this in *After Whiteness*, it relates to his argument since gender-based and sexualized violence are tools of racism and colonialism, including for some Christian missions. Indian Residential Schools in Canada and American Indian boarding schools are primary examples. The rates of sexual violence in Indian Residential Schools in Canada, many of which were run by churches, were astronomical, perhaps as high as 75 percent in some schools.[16] Sexual violence was used as a tool to subdue and conquer. It is a history of power as domination. This sexual violence also tells a story about sexual

---

missions (Kelly Brown Douglas, *Sexuality and the Black Church: A Womanist Perspective* [Maryknoll: Orbis, 1999]).

16 Joanna Rice, "Indian Residential School Truth and Reconciliation Commission of Canada," *Cultural Survival Quarterly Magazine* (March, 2011), accessed February 27,

desires and fantasies, of sexual ethics and theologies that either enabled such violence or were completely ignored with little to no accountability. It is a history about power and sexuality.[17] Again, these histories of inequality and these discourses[18] about sexuality are part of the situatedness of theological education and, as Jennings reminds us, need to be named and actively resisted today.

Similar Christian discourses on sexuality (i.e., those steeped in top-down power and theological understandings of some people and bodies as more sexual and sinful than others) continue to this day and add to the distorted formation of students for witness and discipleship. Examples include anti-LGBTQ+ arguments and policies; the continued sexualization of women's bodies, Black women's bodies, and indigenous women's bodies, whose sexuality was understood as sinful; complementarian views of gender as binary (male and female); arguments promoting sexual purity, including (especially) women's virginity; and "abstinence-only" policies and arguments.

Each of these needs to be unpacked in detail. Given the constraints of this paper, it will suffice to say that what they all have in common is that they contribute to feelings of shame, which increases the likelihood for low self-esteem and abuse. When sexual and gender minorities are denied their humanity and belovedness, they experience deep shame for being themselves. That shame can make them vulnerable to abuse as sexual predators seek out those who are vulnerable.[19] For those who are not minorities, or those who have greater social

---

2022, https://www.culturalsurvival.org/publications/cultural-survival-quarterly/indian-residential-school-truth-and-reconciliation.

17 In the colonial imagination, indigenous bodies are also associated with sexual sin. As Robert Warrior explains, indigenous peoples were often likened to the biblical Canaanites by Christian colonizers—worthy of mass destruction because of sexual sin. In the Bible, the Canaanites commit acts of sexual violence in Sodom (Gen 19:1–29) and prostituted themselves before their gods (Gen 28:21–22, Deut 28:18, 1 Kings 14:24). In the eyes of the colonizers, indigenous peoples were considered sexually perverse. They associated indigenous nakedness with sin, lust, and shame and considered their bodies dirty and sexually violable—"rapable." Sexual violence is part of the colonial legacy of Christian missions (Andrea Smith, *Conquest: Sexual Violence and American Indian Genocide* [Durham: Duke, 2015], 10).

18 The notion of "discourse" comes from history, historiography, and cultural studies in the work of philosopher Michel Foucault. It includes "ways of constituting knowledge, together with the social practices, forms of subjectivity and power relations which inhere in such knowledges and relations between them. Discourses are more than ways of thinking and producing meaning. They constitute the 'nature' of the body, unconscious and conscious mind and emotional life of the subjects they seek to govern" (Chris Weedon, *Feminist Practice and Post-Structuralist Theory* [Oxford: Basil Blackwell,1987], 108).

19 Hilary Jerome Scarsella and Stephanie Krehbiel, "Sexual Violence: Christian Theological Legacies and Responsibilities," *Religion Compass* 13, (Sept 2019): 1–13, 4.

privilege—such as heterosexual white men—feelings of sexual shame for simply being human or for having experienced sexual abuse themselves, can contribute to a lack of self-awareness and other-awareness that can increase their risk for committing sexual abuse.[20]

These discourses that produce sexual shame illustrate how theology can participate in systems of sexual violence.[21] Reiterating this point and making the connection to Christianity's historical legacy of distorted formation, Hilary Jerome Scarsella and Stephanie Krehbiel, feminist scholars and advocates for survivors of sexual violence, state:

> Sexual violence is perpetrated disproportionately against those whose perceived worth is historically precarious: women, people of color, LGBTQIA+ people, people with disabilities, people who are incarcerated, detained, undocumented, or without a home. The precarity that attends these social locations can be traced, in part, to Christianity's clear history of associating sin with particular kinds of bodies: women's bodies, black and brown bodies, LGBTQIA+ bodies, disabled bodies, criminalized bodies.[22]

The distorted formation that takes place within theological education has been and continues to be situated within Christian attitudes and discourses related to sexuality as it intersects also with narratives related to race, class, ability, etcetera. Therefore, a commitment at theological schools to formation for witness and discipleship that is peace- and justice-focused will need to examine these discourses and promote a moral vision of nonviolent and life-giving (intersectional) sexuality for all.

As a feminist scholar, I begin this work of naming and resisting unhealthy views of sexuality by listening to those who have been harmed by them. Along with feminist scholar Sarah Ahmed, I find that complaints of abuses of power are an excellent place to hear these voices. In *Complaint!*, to better reveal how institutions use power to stop these complaints from being brought forward and/or to ignore them when they are, Ahmed listens with a feminist ear to those who have experienced sexual harassment in postsecondary education.

---

20 There are many reasons why people sexually offend. From a survey of the research, and from what is known about sexual offenders, W. L. Marshall, D. Anderson, and F. Champaigne propose that self-esteem plays a role in the reasons for sexual offending—specifically, that low self-esteem may contribute to this behavior ("Self-esteem and Its Relationship to Sexual Offending," *Psychology, Crime & Law* 3, no. 3 (1997): 161–86). Therefore, religious stories and teachings about sexuality that produce feelings of shame, which lower self-esteem, are part of the problem.

21 Hilary Jerome Scarsella, "Victimization via Ritualization: Christian Communion and Sexual Abuse," *Trauma and Lived Religion: Transcending the Ordinary*, eds. R. Ruard Ganzevoort and Srdjan Sremac et al. (Switzerland: Palgrave Macmillan, 2019): 225–52.

22 Scarsella and Krehbiel, "Sexual Violence," 4.

Only some people are considered "complainers," Ahmed reminds us. "Don't complain!" we are taught regularly as children. To be called a complainer is a bad thing, and "to be heard as complaining is not to be heard."[23] People are dismissed as "complainers" since complaining is to be stuck on being negative.

To find where distorted views of sexuality, race, and gender continue in theological education today, listen to complaints about related abuses of power, because, as Ahmed states, "To cover up a complaint is to cover over what the complaint was about." In Ahmed's research, these complaints were about the "sexist and ableist bullying, the 'sexism that is rampant' within universities."[24]

But how is all this related to the formation of students for witness and discipleship? To answer this question, I turn to ethnographic researcher and practical theologian, Marilyn Naidoo. What Naidoo makes explicit, that could only be gleaned from Jennings and Ahmed, is that institutional culture plays a significant role in theological formation, or formation for witness and discipleship. For this reason, paying attention to institutional culture as well as what is taught in the classroom is important if we are invested in formation for witness and service to the church and society. Culture, she explains, "refers to processors, categories and knowledge through which a community is defined (Donald & Rattansi 1992). Students are formed by [an] institution's culture as they interact with it and with others in the learning context, which functions as a plausibility structure for nurturing and sustaining the culture's shared meanings and symbols (Geertz 1973)."[25]

The continuing legacy of inequality and unjust power dynamics regarding race in South Africa, as well as little being known about how theological institutions handle diversity and the implications for student formation, prompted Naidoo's research.[26] Her aims were to better understand how future ministers are being prepared to handle issues of diversity and to assess the critical role of the theological institution's culture in relation to student formation on the topic of diversity (i.e., issues of race, ethnicity, class, gender, and sexual orientation, which have an interlocking nature).[27]

To accomplish these aims, she conducted a two-year ethnographic study of two private Protestant theological institutions in South Africa (spending equal time at each) gaining information through student interviews, focus groups, and staff interviews. Naidoo also gained knowledge of students' experiences by "attending classes, visiting student residences, going to chapel services, attending recreational activities, taking meals with students on and off campus, even

23 Sarah Ahmed, *Complaint!* (Durham: Duke, 2021), 1.

24 Ahmed, 10.

25 Naidoo, "An Ethnographic Study," 2.

26 Naidoo, 1.

27 Naidoo, 1

attending a graduation ceremony." Her goal was to "let the formative process unfold and watch students and staff as they experienced and negotiated their institution's culture."[28]

Naidoo's findings are significant. Both institutions named "diversity" as important, but both failed to link diversity positively to ministerial identity formation in a way that would make a significant difference to how students felt about it. In other words, the institutions promoted diversity in policy but not practice, and this negatively impacted student formation for diversity and equality in ministry. The institutional culture of the Protestant Independent tradition (Institution A), was described as having a "disengaged stance towards diversity issues" with a "colour-blind theology . . . perpetuating surface [level] change."[29] The Protestant Mainline tradition (Institution B) culture included an awareness of diversity as administrators and faculty saw themselves as agents in the transformation of society; however, theirs was a "taken-for-granted" stance—"leaving no reason to discuss that diversity and whether or not it translated into student integration." "The assumption was made," Naidoo explains, that "living in community was sufficient to help students 'rub against' each other. However, formation does not happen by osmosis but is built in community through the integration of personal and community formation (Tatum 1997)."[30]

Naidoo's research suggests that because neither institution lived out its commitment to diversity via institutional culture and community, diversity was not adopted in a meaningful way by students in their ministerial identity formation. While students in both institutions were committed to racial justice and understanding how diverse perspectives could enrich an understanding of the Christian life, "there was generally a culture of silence, as students were afraid to speak because of the fear of being victimised and jeopardising their chances of ordination."[31]

In a more recent article on the significance of institutional culture for student formation, Naidoo reiterates that "the relationship between the faculty, staff and students communicates potent messages about the nature of leadership and community."[32] Through their interactions with and observations of various relationships within the institution, "students rapidly come to understand power relationships within the theological community and subconsciously take

28 Naidoo, 3.

29 Naidoo, 1.

30 Naidoo, 8.

31 Naidoo, 10.

32 Marilyn Naidoo, "Challenging the Status Quo of an Institutional Culture in Theological Training," *Stellenbosch Theological Journal* 3, no. 2 (2017): 493–546, 539.

that model into their work."[33] Looking back at her ethnographic research, in Institution A, for example, where there was an official stance of non-racism, non-sexism, and equal treatment of all, administrators and educators spoke as though these inequalities no longer existed, as did most of the White students. However, in her interviews with Black African students at the same institution, "the topic of race on campus was never far from the surface" but remained difficult to talk about and to change. One student shared, referring to the student population, "I think in everyone's mind there is something about the colour of your skin. We think about this but we cannot speak about it."[34] A culture of "colour-blindness" caused some students to remain unaware of their ongoing White privilege, and caused others to remain silent rather than stand out and be considered a "complainer."[35] Naidoo illustrates some of the ways in which learning is "socially constructed in a reflective practicing community."[36]

Naidoo's findings also reveal that theological institutions form institutional cultures that are more "intense" than those of most other higher education institutions because their cultural script includes intellectual, social, and religious worlds that shape beliefs and practices in the life of the institution.[37] In Institution A, Naidoo found that scriptural resources influenced and shaped student views on diversity through a kind of uncritical biblical literalism and an emphasis on the individual's relationship with God, for example. So, while diversity was technically promoted in institutional policy, social systemic relationships of power remained unexamined in conversation with the Bible and theology. This half-hearted approach did not empower or teach students the skills to name and deconstruct ongoing racism and sexism in regard to their faith, nor to construct a liberating vision of equality that celebrates diversity and is supported by their faith.[38]

Naidoo's findings illustrate the profound connection between institutional culture and faith formation and offer suggestions for how to strengthen formation for ministry that celebrates diversity and equality in practice. If "institutional culture is one of the most salient forces operating within colleges and universities,"[39] then it ought to be carefully considered and taken seriously in theological schools. I agree with her that "within theological education we need to dismantle beliefs and practices that shape and sustain social injustice

---

33 Naidoo, 539–40.

34 Naidoo, "An Ethnographic Study," 4.

35 Naidoo, 2.

36 Naidoo, "Challenging the Status Quo," 539.

37 Naidoo, 532.

38 Naidoo, "An Ethnographic Study," 5.

39 Naidoo, "Challenging the Status Quo," 531.

and that [this] will require some institution[al] cultures to be challenged and changed."[40] With her, I see the importance of "being aware of the formative nature of the institutional culture" as that which "provides critical insights into an institution's change process and can help theological students and educators to find a common theological discourse."[41] When our theological schools do not embody cultures of sexual peace—when silence and secrecy are modeled over transparency regarding complaints of sexual abuse, when a culture of shame exists around sexual and gender diversity and women's pleasure—the burden to form students to be healthy sexual beings in relation to self and others falls to other influential sources in their lives (e.g., family, friends, secular society). Theological schools have a unique and impactful opportunity to form students for sexual peacemaking and peacemaking as sexual persons, but if they fail to do so, they risk doing harm.

Sexing Our Cultures of Peace: Sexual Education and Faith Formation for Peace and Justice

Rather than form students into versions of the "independent white man who seeks control through the accumulation of knowledge and possession," Jennings imagines theological education as formation into a community of belonging. He writes:

> Theological education is supposed to open up sites where we enter the struggle to rethink our people. We think them again, but now with others who must rethink their people. And in this thinking together we begin to see what we had not seen before: we belong to each other, we belong together. Belonging must become the hermeneutic starting point from which we think the social, the political, the individual, the ecclesial, and the most crucial for this work, the educational. Western education (and theological education) as it now exists works against a pedagogy of belonging.[42]

I value Jennings's vision of theological education and want to emphasize its relevance as a vision for all relationships within the institution. Openness to ongoing formation for peace and justice is something that could and should be modeled by all people within the institution in their various roles and relationships to create an institutional culture of belonging—a community of belonging with appreciation for each person and the role they play, including as sexual people. As Jennings argues, whereas Whiteness performed is a "refusal to envision shared facilitation, a refusal to place oneself in the journey of others, a

40 Naidoo, 531.

41 Naidoo, 531.

42 Jennings, *After Whiteness*, 15.

refusal of the vulnerability of a centeredness from below (rather than from the towering heights of whiteness),"[43] a commitment to belonging values formation as still open and teaches a vision of mission and witness that is also open to being formed in relationship/community. Imagine if this were the case regarding sexual identity and faith formation—if cultures of openness and belonging related to sexuality were practiced. What might this look like or include?

I agree with feminist Christian ethicist Kate Ott that we need more conversations about healthy sexuality, including healthy sexuality for professional ethics in ministry, for student formation. Healthy and liberating sexual ethics and understandings of sexuality go beyond "what not to do" as sexual persons. And yes, this is something that needs to be taught and embodied in community life and culture as well as in the classroom. How can this be embodied? This can happen through, for example, transparency as opposed to secrecy; sex-positivity and an emphasis on the importance of mutual pleasure in sexual relationships; an understanding of sexuality not as some separate part of us but always shaping who we are and how we relate to one another as embodied persons; and so on. Whether in the classroom or the institutional culture at large, resisting narratives that perpetuate sexual shame is crucial to promoting healthy sexuality and self-awareness as well as for preventing abuse, and these are some ways we can do that.

I would also suggest that an institution committed to forming sexual people of peace will better prepare students for ministry by offering them a course in professional sexual ethics. Beyond boundaries, Ott offers a theological reflection on sexuality and sexual health underpinned by scripture and tradition for sexual ethics for people going into ordained ministry.[44] Her ethic is informed by biblical understandings of creation, incarnation, and the love commandment that affirm our created goodness as sexual people and the importance of us being self- and other-regarding people in our sexuality. Her work is a valuable resource.

Conclusion

Jennings's contributions are essential for Anabaptist-Mennonite theological schools and their administrators and faculty if we seek to form students for ministry and witness who are committed to peace and justice. As Jennings reiterates, theological formation is contextual and informed by existing histories and relationships of unequal power, as are the contexts for ministry. If the colonial

---

43 Jennings, 101.

44 Kate Ott, "Sexuality, Health, and Integrity," *Professional Sexual Ethics: A Holistic Ministry Approach*, eds. Patricia Beattie Jung and Darryl W. Stephens (Minneapolis: Fortress, 2013), 14.

nature of Western education is not named, then its values—including possession, control, mastery, and self-sufficiency—will continue to be performed and promoted within our theological schools and, in turn, shape the churches and witness work that our students participate in. This competitive, controlling, individualistic mindset is antithetical to the good news understood as God's love for all of us, and to the work of giving and receiving this good news through Christian witness. As I have argued, this is especially true with regard to sexuality, as well as the intersections between sexuality and other social locations (e.g., race, gender).

Our postsecondary institutions are historically located and cannot escape the current power inequalities within the academy, church, and society today. However, I have faith and hope that we can nevertheless do more to resist such inequalities by conscientizing ourselves to these harmful narratives and by listening to those who voice complaints. This will enable us to better embody cultures of peace and justice as sexual people and form one another for witness and discipleship in service for the church and society.

Formed for Witness by the Biblical Story

Anabaptist Congregations Engaging the Narrative Lectionary

Jennifer Davis Sensenig

More than a century ago, mathematician Henri Poincaré observed: "Science is built up of facts, as a house is built of stones; but an accumulation of facts is no more science than a heap of stones is a house."[1] When it comes to our engagement with scripture, let us likewise not be content with an accumulation of facts or a pile of stones. Let us notice how the composition and set of each stone or story might relate to the whole. The Spirit of Christ through Joshua invites us to ask, "What mean these stones?"[2] Let us imagine future generations at home in the scriptures, who freely move into the public arena well-equipped for witness, come what may.

Toward this vision, I will analyze and summarize in this article the results of interviews with North American Anabaptist pastors who have used the Narrative Lectionary as their preaching and/or teaching texts for a year or more. I will integrate their practical experience of using the Narrative Lectionary with my argument that as a tool for congregational formation in the biblical story it is particularly well suited to Anabaptist-oriented congregations and deserves an even broader embrace among our preachers and other Christian formation leaders. Finally, I suggest that a congregation who year-by-year engages the whole story of scripture is spiritually strengthened and better positioned for the congregational discernment and adaptive action that Christian witness requires.

Jennifer Davis Sensenig earned an MDiv from Anabaptist Mennonite Biblical Seminary in 1998 and has since served as a pastor in three Mennonite Church USA congregations, most currently Community Mennonite Church (Harrisonburg, VA). She enjoys making music, reading novels, and gardening with her spouse and primary dialogue partner on all things biblical.

1 Henri Poincaré, *Science and Hypothesis*, trans. William Hohn Greenstreet (New York: Walter Scott, 1905), 141, as quoted in Francis Su, *Mathematics for Human Flourishing* (New Haven, CT: Yale University Press, 2020), 38.

2 Josh 4:21, more commonly rendered, "What do these stones mean?"

To be clear, a lectionary doesn't do the work of congregational formation in the biblical story, but in the hands of well-equipped congregational leaders a lectionary can make the work easier and improve the learning, growth, and encounter that is possible when a community gathers in the Spirit of Christ to learn the logic of their sacred story.[3] If one of our aims is to form congregations who are at home in the biblical story and readily see the resonances between the message of scripture and their contemporary trauma, economy, politics, family, faith, and watershed, then the Narrative Lectionary may be a better choice for some congregations than the Revised Common Lectionary.

Called to Be a Servant of the Word: A Glorious and Formidable Task

I am a leader of congregational formation in the biblical story. I share this responsibility with many others in the congregation I serve, including other pastors and teachers, as well as worship, prayer, and song leaders. I also share this responsibility with the ecumenical pastoral reading group with whom I study lectionary scriptures each week. Further, I practice and develop gifts and skills for biblical storytelling through the Network of Biblical Storytellers International and a local guild using the same method for sharing biblical stories.[4]

I understand my particular gifts and calling in relation to a sixteenth-century Anabaptist description of pastors as Servants of the Word.[5] I also recognize that formation in the biblical story where I currently live, in Virginia, is indebted to the enslaved brothers and sisters who heard and interpreted God's

3 I have been blessed in my years of pastoral ministry to partner with many gifted congregational leaders. I especially want to name a few who did not have formal theological education yet labored with keen sensitivity to the scriptures: Ellen Miller, a worship and prayer leader at Cedar Falls (IA) Mennonite Church; Eddie Beres, a worship leader at Pasadena (CA) Mennonite Church; and Jeremy Nafziger, Greg Yoder, and Angie Clemens, music leaders at Community Mennonite Church (Harrisonburg, VA).

4 The mission of the network (see https://www.nbsint.org/about/history/) is "to encourage everyone to learn and tell biblical stories." Two websites that introduce this method are nbsint.org and gotell.org.

5 The German moniker *Diener des Wortes* (servant of the word) became popular among sixteenth-century European Anabaptists for their leaders who were not primarily priests (per the Roman Catholic church, administering the sacraments) nor state-sanctioned pastors (per the magisterial Reformers, minding a flock) but rather leaders charged to equip folks for interpreting and living the scriptures with the guidance of the Holy Spirit.

word as a counter testimony to the dominant interpretation of white enslavers, from whom I am a direct descendant.[6]

> Deprived of literacy—reading and writing—the enslaved people too came to knowledge of God, of God's will and purpose, and intimate knowledge of God's Son Jesus through hearing. The enslaved people listened as they stood near the open windows of churches or parlors. They talked and prayed and ruminated among themselves under the boughs of hush arbors, in thickets, or in rude cabins. They prayed silently at day during work in the fields, cried out in hurt at dark midnight. The enslaved people entrusted to memory and heart miracle stories and parables, events and sayings, names and places from the Hebrew Scriptures and Christian Testament. . . . In the opaque enigma of their enslavement, the people prayed and sang and praised the God whom they believed would break the slavery chain at last.[7]

For me, preaching and teaching the scriptures in fulfillment of a life-time calling as a Servant of the Word and in response to the genuine desire of God's people is both a glorious and a formidable task. Forming people in the way of Christ through engagement with scripture, one another, and the missional opportunities of a particular host community requires regular adaptation to new conditions as well as seasons of inquiry and refreshment for those of us called to lead the church. Those who share a similar calling might be familiar with the following conditions that folks in my congregation periodically describe:

- "I grew up in the church and went to Sunday school, but I still don't see how the Bible hangs together."
- "I didn't grow up in the church, so I've heard some Bible stories and have some favorite verses, but I don't have a sense for the whole story."
- "I don't read the Bible much. I don't get much out of it when I do. I'm worried I won't be able to teach my own children or groups within the congregation."

The holy ground where I labor is a congregation.[8] Among us are Bible scholars as well as folks who have never read the Bible. We are children, youth, and adults of all ages and degrees of engagement in congregational life. We are mostly white. One of the thorny problems our congregation encounters in Christian formation is equipping each generation and all ages of believers with a sense of the whole biblical story. When we know our sacred story and can draw on its themes, wisdom, and trajectory for being and sharing good news with the

---

6 My eighth-great grandfather enslaved hundreds of African women and men at the Westover plantation on the James River.

7 M. Shawn Copeland, *Knowing Christ Crucified: The Witness of African American Religious Experience* (Maryknoll, NY: Orbis, 2018), 33.

8 I've been serving as lead pastor of Community Mennonite Church (Harrisonburg, VA) since 2008.

world, our individual and collective lives make more sense. Put more precisely, "If we are to find God, we will do so in a story."[9]

In this introduction to the Narrative Lectionary, I show how it might serve as a tool for congregational formation in the biblical story.[10] I will not resolve our congregations' formation problem so that we Christian formation leaders can move on to something else. Indeed, I do not wish to move on. Formation and witness are not sequential operations of the Christian life. Our settings for witness (i.e., a neighborhood without sufficient affordable housing; a planet experiencing climate crisis; a polis dependent upon migrant and immigrant labor; a school district lacking teachers, bus drivers, and food security) inform our formation practices, including our reading and interpretation of the Bible.[11] Likewise, our sense of God's word in scripture informs our capacity for witness. Just as Jesus told the same parable more than once in developing riffs of verbal explanation and lived embodiment, Christian formation leaders persevere in our creative labor from one generation to the next in response to new conditions for witness.

My longing for my own ministry and that of other Christian formation leaders is that in the Spirit of Christ we might form communities who can recognize our stories in God's story as we make fitting analogies and draw insight from scripture for living well in the light of Christ.[12] My engagement with scripture includes pondering, puzzling, and connecting scriptures with each other and with our lives as Christian communities. Like the argument by Francis Su that mathematics is necessarily about relationships, that mathematics is "the

---

9 Melissa Florer-Bixler, *Fire by Night: Finding God in the Pages of the Old Testament* (Harrisonburg, VA: Herald, 2019) 160.

10 In the American Evangelical publishing world, a product called *The Story* ostensibly pursues a similar goal of equipping congregations with the big Story of the Bible. I'm not recommending this resource, however. In contrast to *The Story*, the Narrative Lectionary is completely free, and the interpretation and theological emphases are more likely to reflect the preaching/teaching traditions, innovations, and creativity of the congregations using it as opposed to foreclosing the range of meanings to attract the American Evangelical market.

11 Luke 10:25–42—from the lawyer's inquiry to the parable of neighbor love, and from Martha's inquiry to Jesus's defense of Mary's choice—is an example of how word and witness are interlaced in Jesus's ministry.

12 The theory of Human Systems Dynamics—with its appreciation for uncertain and changing conditions, fresh questions, and improvisation based on wise practice—has been useful for me in thinking about how knowing God's story in scripture relates to our Christian witness in the world. A good introduction to this systems theory is Glenda H. Eoyang and Royce J. Holladay, *Adaptive Action: Leveraging Uncertainty in Your Organization* (Stanford, CA: Stanford Business, 2013).

science of patterns and the art of engaging the meaning in those patterns," my vocation as a Christian formation leader is also rooted in a patterned truth.[13]

The weekly work of tending to the scriptures and the Spirit of Christ, such that I can best equip our congregation for Christian witness, is why I am still a congregational pastor after twenty-three years. Like the Apostle Paul, who at times piles on the metaphors, I'm inclined to add the image of a fire to mathematical patterns and stone masonry:

> Planning for corporate worship is like building a campfire. Just as we gather the kindling for a fire, we need to choose carefully our Bible portions for worship. As we plan the prayers, the hymns and the songs, we need to let in plenty of space and air. Too many words without silences between will make our worship fire smoke and choke.
>
> The sticks and logs for the worship fire are the Bible verses. Just as the kindling and the wood can't make themselves into a fire, so the words of the Bible have no power in themselves. They are not alive. Only as the breath of God sets the fire alight can the words of the divine *Word* communicate. Only then can they burn and purge, warm and lighten our lives.[14]

Mennonites and Lectionaries

In C. Arnold Snyder's *Following the Footsteps of Christ: The Anabaptist Tradition*, the chapter on Anabaptist Spiritual Disciplines includes a shimmering section heading: "Living the Bible." My understanding is that while some sixteenth-century Anabaptists leaned toward "living the Bible" as a restorationist impulse of returning to the early church, others were "living the Bible" by immersing themselves in the biblical witness so as to develop adaptive action relevant to their own times and diverse settings. "The common mark of surviving Anabaptist court testimonies is the thoroughly biblical nature of the defenses provided by Anabaptist prisoners, regardless of whether they were women or men, educated or uneducated, literate or illiterate."[15]

While I cannot provide a thorough history of Mennonite use of lectionaries as aids to congregations "living the Bible," a few examples are instructive, beginning with the *Biblical Concordance of the Swiss Brethren, 1540* and *Guide to Holy Scripture*. These two resources confirm that early Anabaptists were in-

---

13 Francis Su, *Mathematics for Human Flourishing*, 44.

14 Eleanor Kreider, *Enter His Gates: Fitting Worship Together* (Scottdale, PA: Herald, 1990), 89.

15 C. Arnold Snyder, *Following the Footsteps of Christ: The Anabaptist Tradition* (Maryknoll, NY: Orbis, 2004), 118.

terested in a rigorous engagement with the Bible.[16] The *Concordance* is arranged topically beginning with Fear of God and including such topics as Rebirth, Bearing Witness, Patience, Alms, Righteousness, Sacrifice, Humility, Treasure, Do Not Worry, Greed, Political Authority, and Child Rearing. It does not include exposition of these topics. Rather, it simply points preachers and teachers to relevant scriptures, at times quoting those scriptures at length. Similarly, the *Guide* is arranged by topic, though alphabetically (in the original German), and includes subheadings directing congregational formation leaders to scriptures throughout the canon.[17] From my twenty-first-century vantage point, these publications—simple tools for rigorous engagement with the scripture—suggest a profound trust in the work of the Holy Spirit among leaders and their congregations who are using them.

In addition to these scripture resource volumes, testimony from *The Martyr's Mirror* highlights Christians in the Anabaptist stream of the church recognizing the performative power of the divine voice in scripture and organizing their congregations to wield this power by knowing and speaking the scriptures—by "living the Bible." Similarly, after citing a litany of Old Testament references, the author of Hebrews asks rhetorically, "Are not all [of them] spirits in the divine service, sent to serve for the sake of those who are to inherit salvation" (Hebrews 1:14)? Yes, this means that the author of Hebrews interprets Old Testament texts as pointing toward Jesus. It seems to also mean that the texts themselves are spiritual companions, not unlike the individuals named in Hebrews chapter 11. The Anabaptist desire for deeply knowing scripture, gaining familiarity with the texts and characters as spiritual companions, may be likened to the affection for and communion with the saints that other streams of Christian faith cultivate.

A twentieth-century example of Mennonite use of lectionaries comes from the North American Mennonite context. In a 1989 churchwide survey by the Mennonite Board of Congregational Ministries (MBCM), pastors were asked what kind of worship resources they wanted the church to publish.[18] Of the more than 400 pastors who responded, roughly 80 percent said they want-

---

16 Both volumes were published under the title *Biblical Concordance of the Swiss Brethren, 1540*, trans. Gilbert Fast and Galen A. Peters (Kitchener, ON: Pandora, 2001).

17 For example, under the topic "Cross," there are subheadings for "All true believers encounter the cross and suffering," "The cross is imposed by God on the faithful," "Through the cross one comes to a knowledge of God," "Carry the cross with patience and gladness," The cross protects the faithful," and "Comfort in the cross of suffering." Each subheading directs readers to relevant scriptures from both the Old Testament and the New Testament (*Biblical Concordance*, 127).

18 I'm indebted to Marlene Kropf both as my former professor and because she welcomed an interview that is the basis of this section.

ed worship resources for the church year. The new denominational Minister of Worship at the time, Marlene Kropf, was surprised, as were the MBCM staff—both because of a high survey response rate and because observing the full cycle of the traditional liturgical year (Advent-Christmas-Epiphany and Lent-Easter-Pentecost) was not widespread at that time among North American Mennonite congregations.

Within a few years, MBCM began publishing worship and preaching resources based on the Revised Common Lectionary (RCL), which was published by the ecumenical Consultation on Common Texts. MBCM did not mandate that all pastors preach from the RCL, but by publishing periodic resources—beginning with the liturgical seasons of Lent and Advent—they introduced many Mennonite congregations to the RCL, a three-year cycle of scripture readings for each Sunday (and special days), including Gospel, Old Testament, Psalm, and Epistle readings. At the same time, Kropf began teaching worship courses at Anabaptist Mennonite Biblical Seminary (AMBS),[19] and by the mid-1990s, when I was an MDiv student there, the RCL formed the scriptural touchstone of our chapel worship services and was integrated into required coursework through the Foundations of Worship and Preaching course.[20]

One of MBCM's rationales for choosing the RCL was that it included a Gospel reading for every Sunday. The centrality of the Gospels for Mennonite discipleship, the pattern of Jesus's life and ministry for church witness, and the Christocentric hermeneutic of our Anabaptist forebears made the RCL attractive and fitting. The common assumption (perhaps true) among my mostly Mennonite seminary colleagues in the 1990s was that mid-twentieth-century Mennonite preaching texts were weighted toward the New Testament and toward the Epistles. Thus, the RCL was embraced as a corrective counterweight to the more independent choices of a previous generation of preachers and pastors. Additionally, using the RCL brought Mennonites into more regular ecumenical conversations in their local communities.

Thus, as a result of MBCM's publishing ministry, today Mennonite Church USA and Mennonite Church Canada leaders are generally aware of the RCL, whether or not they in fact use it, and refer to it as "the lectionary." However, there are plenty of other lectionaries in the history of the church, and several

---

19 At the time, the seminary was named Associated Mennonite Biblical Seminary.

20 The Revised Common Lectionary (RCL) was an ecumenical, Protestant revision based on the Roman Catholic lectionary. It is widely used today among mainline congregations. Some readers may be familiar with *Leader* magazine, published by MennoMedia, which includes RCL-based worship planning materials for particular seasons of the church year, especially Advent–Epiphany, Lent, Easter–Pentecost.

have emerged as intentional alternatives to the RCL.[21] The one that caught my attention was the Narrative Lectionary.

The Narrative Lectionary

A lectionary is a heuristic—a handy tool for congregational faith formation rooted in scripture. A lectionary is an imperfect tool, but, as Christians, we are people of the word and need the Bible—its stories and its story—to form us as the church. The people we influence in our congregations and the people who participate in ministries that we lead need help to engage with scripture in ways that form Christian faith and empower our witness. Anabaptist-minded congregations do this work together. And we who are Christian formation leaders—teachers, worship planners, and preachers—whether our work is paid or unpaid, need help to equip the church for knowing our big Story of redemption, salvation, and the good news of peace.

Like the RCL, the Narrative Lectionary is simply a schedule of scripture readings and observes the church year. Developed by Craig Koester and Rolf Jacobson of Luther Seminary, the Narrative Lectionary has its own coherence and differs from the RCL in several ways. First, the Narrative Lectionary is a four-year-cycle of scripture readings—one year longer than the RCL three-year cycle. While it doesn't include every biblical story or even every book of the Bible, it is designed to annually rehearse the whole story of the Bible through worship, preaching, and teaching.

The Narrative Lectionary begins each year on the Sunday after the US civic holiday, Labor Day,[22] with a creation story from Genesis and moves through the grand arc of the Old Testament during the fall. Its selective sweep through the First Testament is narratively sequential. By Advent, the lection for Sunday comes from the prophets—anticipating a breakthrough in Israel's story and the coming of the Messiah. From Christmas through Easter, the Narrative Lectionary follows the life, ministry, death, and resurrection of Jesus through a single Gospel. (There is a Narrative Lectionary year for Matthew, for Mark, for Luke, and for John.) Again, the Gospels are included not in their entirety but read sequentially so that those following along get a sense of the integrity and flow of each Gospel. Then from Easter until Pentecost, the Narrative Lectionary enters the period of the early church as it follows scriptures from Acts and the Epistles.

While the RCL most often pairs Old Testament lections with the Gospel for the day, the Narrative Lectionary aims to engage the Old Testament for

21 Steve Thorngate, "What's the Text? Alternatives to the Common Lectionary," *Christian Century*, October 16, 2013, https://www.christiancentury.org/article/2013-10/what-s-text.

22 The US Labor Day holiday always falls on the first Monday of September. Thus, the Narrative Lectionary begins the following Sunday.

its own sake.[23] Although the RCL was never designed as a menu for preachers with four options per Sunday, it has at times functioned this way in Mennonite congregations. From September through May, the Narrative Lectionary, with just one primary teaching/preaching text for each Sunday, unfurls the biblical story from creation through the early church period. And the typical Narrative Lectionary teaching/preaching text for a Sunday is longer than a typical RCL lection.[24]

Ten Key Findings: Interviews with Anabaptist Preachers Using the Narrative Lectionary

I began preaching and teaching using the Narrative Lectionary in the fall of 2020. As a recipient of a Louisville Institute Pastoral Study Project grant in 2021 while on sabbatical leave,[25] I was able to deepen my understanding of the Narrative Lectionary, develop resources, collect visual art related to the Narrative Lectionary, and interview Anabaptist preachers from the United States and Canada who were using this relatively new lectionary for congregational Christian formation in the biblical story.[26] The titles of the following ten sections of this essay summarize key findings from these interviews.

1. Mennonites are experimenting with the Narrative Lectionary.

The Mennonite pastors I interviewed gave various reasons for trying out the Narrative Lectionary. All of them had experience with the RCL, which they had used regularly but not exclusively for worship and preaching texts in their congregations.

- A pastor whose congregation recently began using the Narrative Lectionary said, "Our local ecumenical group was making the shift. I appre-

---

23 There are seasons when the RCL includes the option of a continuous or sequential reading of portions of the Old Testament, but these are usually in Ordinary Time, when it seems fewer Mennonite congregations use any lectionary.

24 The Narrative Lectionary does include a very short companion text for each week, which I'll address later in this article.

25 I am deeply grateful to Community Mennonite Church (Harrisonburg, VA), the local congregation that has shaped my pastoral ministry the past thirteen years. Their gift of a sabbatical allowed me time for living into my favorite line from *Confession of Faith in a Mennonite Perspective*: "We commit ourselves to persist and delight in reading, studying, and meditating on the Scripture" (Scottdale, PA: Herald, 1995), Article 4. The Louisville Institute grant allowed me to invest in interviewing pastors and leaders, writing retreats, and pursuing artwork and resource development. Without all that the grant afforded me, I would not have been able to share this research in an article for publication.

26 Of the twenty-two pastors I interviewed, eleven were women and eleven were men. Three were BIPOC, and five were reporting on Canadian congregations.

ciated that the Narrative Lectionary was still linked to the Christian year and had a deep dive into each Gospel. My hope is that people will catch the bigger narrative over time."

- Several reported that when using the RCL they typically preached from the Gospel text, even though the RCL provides four scriptures for each Sunday. A common sentiment was: "By using the Narrative Lectionary I realized that my RCL tendency was to preach the Gospel nine out of ten times."
- One preacher who had used the RCL for fifteen years was seeking something fresh to inspire her own preaching. She described her attraction to the Narrative Lectionary this way: "I appreciated the idea of sustained Old Testament continuity rather than texts 'cherry-picked' to match the Gospel. And I was intrigued by the basic concept—four years, with each Gospel having its own year."[27]
- Five pastors commented on the simplicity of having a single scripture for each Sunday already selected rather than investing pastoral or worship committee planning energy around that decision.
- A down-to-earth pastor commented poignantly, "This pandemic year we were scrambling. As a preacher, I was craving . . . needing some structure, a frame, a story. I was craving a Story . . ."
- One pastor explained that the benefit of the Narrative Lectionary for her was stepping into the same narrative stream on sequential Sundays. She found this useful for her own preparation. Likewise, members of her congregation, even when they were absent, were moving along in an unfolding biblical story rather than jumping backward and forward in the biblical narrative.
- Another pastor shared, "My mission in life is to help people learn how to read the Bible. The Narrative Lectionary is less proof-texting, bigger chunks of scripture, and more context than using RCL. And, of course, the narrative arc is the main benefit."

---

27 The RCL is a three-year cycle: Year A (Matthew), Year B (Mark), Year C (Luke). Portions of the Gospel of John are included in the RCL but with less sustained attention. Thus the Narrative Lectionary's Year Four (John) is, for many, an attractive quality of this lectionary.

2. Being at home with the Bible is important for our life of faith.

We are formed by the stories we hear, the stories we tell, and the stories we rediscover in new circumstances.[28] The Bible is full of stories. The Bible is also a Story that hangs together and holds us together as people of the word. Rolf Jacobson, one of the originators of the Narrative Lectionary, emphasized that pastors can be key leaders to champion biblical literacy as important for faith.

Pastors I interviewed had this to say about the role of the Narrative Lectionary in their congregation's life of faith as it related to biblical literacy:

- One seasoned pastor who has now used the Narrative Lectionary in two different congregations had noticed that "people who didn't grow up in the church didn't have basic stories or the storyline of the Bible."
- "I liked the idea of the overarching story improving biblical literacy. I want to nuance that because by biblical literacy I don't mean just being able to name the books of the Bible but to also grow in a love for scripture and to learn the story in a way that is neither legalistic nor literalistic. We want to raise children with the big picture of the Bible."
- "Our congregation is pretty post-Christian, or at least post-Christendom. They don't read the Bible themselves. Sunday is really their only exposure to scripture."
- A pastor who focuses on children and youth faith formation shared, "Our people need 'hooks' onto which to hang biblical stories, characters, and themes. The RCL doesn't provide the hooks. I became an advocate for using the Narrative Lectionary in our congregation because of this concern for biblical literacy."
- A Canadian pastor noticed that older generations had Bible college experience but younger generations did not. "We needed to do some of that biblical literacy work at the congregational level."

While some who have adopted the Narrative Lectionary for preaching and teaching simply hope for greater familiarity with the Bible among their members, some also mentioned the need for discernment. As one pastor pointed out, "Having the perspective of the larger story is better for congregational interpretation and for application of scripture to our contemporary setting."

2. Integrating our preaching/teaching scriptures with other Christian formation opportunities is desirable.

I believe that preachers and other Christian formation leaders—like Sunday school teachers and Bible study leaders—are doing our best work when we collaborate in biblically rooted congregational Christian faith formation. In

28 Narrative psychologist Dan P. McAdams explores redemptive stories in *The Redemptive Self: Stories Americans Live By* (Oxford: Oxford University Press, 2006).

different ministry settings within the same congregation, diverse pastors and program leaders are equipping people of all ages to know the biblical story and recognize themselves as actors in new iterations of the same story today. Thus, using the Narrative Lectionary for both worship/preaching and Christian formation curriculum might be the most effective means of helping congregations become more at home in the biblical story.

Jacobson emphasizes that the congregational experience with the Narrative Lectionary will be improved by also using, if at all possible, the primary preaching text in Christian formation settings beyond worship—especially Bible studies and classes for children, youth, and adults. Several pastors mentioned that while they hear a congregational call for linking children's and adult scriptures on Sunday mornings, loyalty to denominational curriculum can be an obstacle to such integration. "I would love to have Anabaptist Sunday school curriculum where kids were tracking with Narrative Lectionary scriptures," said one of those pastors. Another pastor, longing for more staff, said, "I have some shame as a pastor when I think of how our worship/preaching texts don't match what is happening in our children's curriculum. How could we do something more coordinated? I'm looking at more of my time as a pastor focused on children and believe that something that connects with worship [scripture texts] is ideal."

In the course of my interviews, I found three Mennonite congregations who purchased curriculum linked to the Narrative Lectionary for their Christian formation programs for children and youth. All commended the quality of the curriculum and the ability of their teachers to highlight Anabaptist emphases in their classes. Another congregation who purchased a different curriculum linked to the Narrative Lectionary was less satisfied with the quality of the material.

4. Preachers (and congregations) appreciate hearing the good news from the Old Testament.[29]

While one preacher reported that his congregation's worship commission thought there was "too much Old Testament" in their first year using the Narrative Lectionary, nearly every other pastor reported that their congregations were eager to dig into stories that had seldom been part of their worship/preaching diet. They shared the following sentiments regarding the lectionary's fall focus on the Old Testament:

---

29 Florer-Bixler's *Fire by Night: Finding God in the Pages of the Old Testament* is an excellent example of one preacher's discoveries and practice of preaching from the Old Testament. She states, "The story of God's faithful love, interrupted by human disobedience, is written so that each of us becomes a character in it. This story is to be read from the inside out, as we push and pull at the narratives, argue with the characters, demand an answer from our enemies and heroes and even from God" (181).

- "Shadrach, Meshach, and Abednego; Jacob at the river before he reconciles with Esau—people think these are children's stories, but there are things we [adults also] need in there."
- "Where is the good news? That's an important question to keep in mind and wrestle with no matter which part of scripture is in focus for preaching/teaching."
- "I love how the Narrative Lectionary invites us into the whole biblical story and helps us look at how the Old Testament connects with Jesus, but not in a way that diminishes the integrity of the First Testament." Because of the narrative chronology, "this lectionary helps with meta-thinking about the editing and how the scriptures were compiled—both the chronology of events and when in Israel's history these stories were compiled."
- One seasoned pastor admitted that her RCL habit was to preach on the Gospel reading. By contrast, she described her first year's experience with the Narrative Lectionary and preaching from the Old Testament during the fall as "life-altering." She shared that she and her congregation have found the Old Testament "so relevant" and "more resonant than ever before."
- Finally, one interviewee summarized the value of focusing on the Old Testament each fall this way: "Theologically, this helps us with 1) understanding ourselves as the people of God, 2) recognizing collective sin, 3) recognizing God's grace for all people, and 4) critiquing nationalism through the dynamic between kings and prophets."

5. We value a sustained, sequential reading of each Gospel.

Many pastors I interviewed affirmed in one way or another the sustained, sequential reading of the Gospels over the Narrative Lectionary's four-year cycle. One pastor said, "I've fallen in love with a Gospel every year." Her congregation has twice divided up the year's Gospel, with folks learning a section by heart and then presenting the whole Gospel at a special biblical storytelling event. Another pastor who likewise affirmed the centrality of the sustained Gospel readings commented, "The idea that Anabaptists are uniquely Jesus-centered in their reading/interpretation of scripture is a fallacy, but the Narrative Lectionary's focus on a Gospel each year is great."

Many of the pastors also specifically mentioned the opportunity to focus on the life, ministry, death, and resurrection of Jesus through the lens of one Gospel each year and especially appreciated having a year to focus on John, the Gospel that, in the RCL, is quite abridged and scattered across the three years. In addition, Craig Koester, a New Testament scholar and another originator of the Narrative Lectionary, pointed out a specific benefit to reading the Gospel of Mark sequentially: "When you hear Mark 13 (the 'little apocalypse') in sequence, it's immediately before Christ's passion. So [in the Narrative Lectionary] you hear Jesus's arrest, trial, and crucifixion as the apocalyptic event in Mark's Gospel."

Another pastor reiterates: "What's been most valuable for us has been preaching through a whole Gospel. As the main preacher, I begin reading in the fall to prepare for the Christmas-Easter series." Jacobson challenges members of congregations to read the year's Gospel on their own during the period from Christmas to Easter. For many people, he notes, it's the first time they are challenged to read a Gospel straight through, which can be transformative for their faith.

6. You might not like the Narrative Lectionary.

I grew up in a stream of the church that did not use a lectionary—the Baptist General Conference.[30] After graduating from college I enrolled in seminary to learn (all over again) how to read the Bible, and I chose biblical studies as my academic concentration in the MDiv program. My first exposure to a lectionary (RCL) was troubling: *Who chose these texts? Why does the lection begin or end where it does? What about texts that don't show up in the lectionary? And how will folks appreciate the beauty of the big biblical picture if we bounce around rather than sustain a closer reading of each book?*

Some of these questions persist for me decades later, even with the use of the Narrative Lectionary, which is preferable (in my mind) for forming congregations in the biblical story. Several pastors likewise expressed hesitations and critiques: One pastor lamented that after using the Narrative Lectionary he wanted more lections from Exodus: "There's so much I want to preach from Exodus!" Another pastor who had used the Narrative Lectionary for two years said, "For us, thirteen weeks of Old Testament was a good challenge, though the arcs were not as useful as I thought they might be. I didn't want to do the work of filling in gaps." Another commented bluntly, "Narrative Lectionary didn't give me enough Acts!" One pastor who noticed his congregation didn't have a personal scripture-reading culture, switched to the Narrative Lectionary after having preached from the RCL for most of four years. A couple years into the switch, however, he hadn't noticed any "aha moments" among members.

If as a Christian formation leader you really want options for preaching—which is how most Mennonites seem to use the RCL—then you may be frustrated with the Narrative Lectionary since there is only one main scripture for each Sunday. The same pastor who had switched to the Narrative Lectionary after four years also missed the "choice" that the RCL presented among four scriptures and the challenge of deciding which scriptures to pair. While he loved

30 This historically Swedish Baptist denomination is now known as Converge. See https://converge.org/.

"the linear progression of the Narrative Lectionary," he described himself as "a synthetic thinker" who also loves to "bring two texts together in my sermons." And, for those who desire an in-depth book study, the Narrative Lectionary will not satisfy your itch.

Reactions were also mixed regarding the Narrative Lectionary's role during special seasons of the Christian calendar year such as Advent. One pastor was thrilled to have a Narrative Lectionary text from Daniel during Advent, seeing it as an opportunity to glimpse the kingdom heralded by the anticipated Messiah. Several others, however, found that the Narrative Lectionary scriptures from the prophets challenged their worship sensibilities during "Christmasy" Advent seasons. And some simply missed the RCL Advent lections they had come to treasure.

7. Congregational, denominational, and ecumenical collaboration strengthens formation in the biblical story.

When I interviewed former denominational leader Marlene Kropf, she offered a query for congregations using the Narrative Lectionary: "With whom could you collaborate to make the use of this lectionary a shared experience across generations in the congregation?" She also registered the need for collaboration at the denominational level, so that published materials integrate worship/preaching scriptures with curriculum for Christian formation across age groups.

My interviews with pastors corroborated this need among Mennonites for fresh collaboration at both the congregational and denominational levels. While this represents a challenge to our existing internal patterns in publishing, the pastors I interviewed reflected deep appreciation for ecumenical collaboration around the Narrative Lectionary. They reported having developed a sense of being in partnership to form congregations in light of the biblical story through the following: (1) participating in one of the Narrative Lectionary Facebook groups, (2) meeting in geographical clusters of pastoral peers for study, (3) connecting with pastoral colleagues from differing cultural/language groups, and (4) listening to podcasts focused on the Narrative Lectionary texts.

In addition, this past year several Mennonite pastors in the United States hosted a virtual pulpit exchange using Narrative Lectionary scriptures. In their respective interviews, these pastors affirmed the value of knowing that their congregations had all been focusing on the same sequence of Bible stories. This pulpit exchange experiment prompted one pastor to query, "I wonder what a collectivist experience of Anabaptists using the Narrative Lectionary might be like. What would the Anabaptist-Mennonite conversation be like? How might it serve/supplement our ministries?" Another pastor summarized his experience saying, "The opportunity to collaborate with an ecumenical group of local pastors on both regular preaching prep and seasonal thematic discussions has been the highlight of the whole Narrative Lectionary experience and the greatest benefit for me."

Nearly every pastor shared that they had shifted at their own initiative to the Narrative Lectionary for preaching, though they also routinely consulted with worship planners and other leaders.

8. Language matters; we don't have to say "lectionary."

Most adults in our congregations wouldn't be able to define the term *lectionary*. One pastor quipped that even in church meetings, the word "lectionary" is a conversation stopper. For most congregational members, if there is a Bible passage presented during worship and a sermon based on that same passage, they aren't going to notice what, if any, lectionary is behind the scenes. Thus, one pastor introduced the Narrative Lectionary without referring to it directly: "I called it a Bible reading plan. Our focus was, 'A Year through the Story of Scripture.'" Another pastor said, "We called our first Narrative Lectionary year 'God's Story, Our Story.' During that year we also told the story of our congregation."

In general, I heard pastors frequently use terms such as *story*, *God's story*, *sacred story*, *narrative*, *shape*, *arc*, and *trajectory* to convey that the Bible is not simply a collection of "readings" but a grand whole. One compelling image emerged from the pastor who said, "I've described what we're doing with the Narrative Lectionary as developing a wide wingspan, including both testaments, understanding ancient scrolls, and getting a view of the whole Bible."

9. Summer breaks are a typical congregational reality.

One of the charms of the Narrative Lectionary is that it carries congregations from creation to Pentecost each year during the seasons when most North American congregations have their highest level of worship attendance—the Sunday after Labor Day through Pentecost in late May or early June. Then congregations tend to adjust to summer schedules.

Some worship planners and preachers love the opportunity to design their own thematic worship series that meet the needs of their congregation for the summer months. For others, the Narrative Lectionary provides some short modules (four–six weeks) that focus on books of the Bible that get less treatment in the four-year cycle.[31]

Nearly everyone I interviewed mentioned that flexibility during these summer months made sense for their congregational rhythms. A few also mentioned

---

31 This past summer my own congregation used a short Narrative Lectionary series on Ephesians, one on Psalms, and a short series that we designed ourselves to focus on the ministries of each of our commissions, with scripture selected by commission leaders.

the value of being "created anew" each fall when congregations begin again with creation stories in Genesis.

10. Give it a whirl.

Speaking as elders in these interviews, both Kropf and Koester independently encouraged preachers to consider a new lectionary if such a tool would energize them and their congregations in terms of engaging the whole biblical story. And more than one preacher mentioned that their own boredom or desire for change was motivation enough to try the Narrative Lectionary. (Who wants to hear from a bored preacher?!) Comments included the following:

- "If you're looking for something new after using the RCL for a while, I would encourage other congregations to consider this lectionary because it understands the Bible as a story—and getting the continuity of the story is important."
- "If we're digging into the word in scripture and connecting to God's Word in Jesus, then we're doing the right thing. If the Narrative Lectionary is a framework for creativity, then run with it. It's fantastic. If it is restrictive or burdensome, then hold it lightly."
- "Because of reports from our worship commission, some in our congregation who didn't know how scriptures were selected for worship noticed that we were using a different lectionary. I think it was good for our congregation to realize that we could try the Narrative Lectionary. We don't have to use the RCL. It loosened us up a bit."

If you're interested in using the Narrative Lectionary in your own congregation, most congregations begin either in September or January. If you begin in the fall, you'll follow Old Testament stories, and then from Christmas to Easter you'll follow a single Gospel sequentially. If you begin in the New Year, you'll start by following a Gospel.

As a tool for congregational formation in the biblical story, the Narrative Lectionary has clearly been useful for some Anabaptist-minded preachers and pastors. The following four sections describe additional benefits reported by leaders using the Narrative Lectionary.

Additional Benefits of Using the Narrative Lectionary

1. The Spirituality of the Companion Texts

The Narrative Lectionary has a very grassroots conception story.[32] It began with Craig Koester experimenting in congregational and seminary settings with a

---

32 I'm grateful to both Rolf Jacobson and Craig Koester for allowing me to interview them in order to assemble the story.

series of scriptures to help folks get the big picture of the Bible. He used maps, photos of the Middle East from his travels and research, and music to enhance his teaching. He also proposed the general format of the Narrative Lectionary (the whole biblical story on the Sundays September through May) at a gathering of pastors. After one of his presentations, a pastor approached Koester saying that he and another eleven pastors were ready to give it a try if Koester would supply the schedule of scripture readings.

Early in its development, the Narrative Lectionary truly had just one scripture reading for each Sunday, but some Episcopalians who were eager to try this emerging lectionary shared that in their liturgical tradition they needed to have a passage from one of the Gospels read in worship every Sunday in order to share the Eucharist. Thus, the Narrative Lectionary added a very short Gospel reading for each of the autumn (Old Testament) Sundays as well as the spring Sundays that focus on Acts or Epistles.

Rolf Jacobson, Old Testament scholar and Koester's collaborator, explained that these selections were hermeneutical decisions.[33] When a Gospel reading is the main scripture in the Narrative Lectionary (from Christmas through Easter), a short passage from the Psalms serves as a companion text. Jacobson, who chose these passages, explained that he intended to highlight major themes in the psalms, including some themes omitted from RCL Psalm lections. Thus, using the Narrative Lectionary today, congregations can always include a Gospel reading in their worship life, even when a Gospel is not the primary teaching/preaching text.

In my interviews with pastors, I did not directly inquire about their congregations' use of the companion texts. My own experience is that because these texts are short they are often inspiration for prayer lines, the frame for a call to worship, or visual arts. When a short Gospel text is a companion for a main reading from the Old Testament, it often provides a potential Christocentric comment on the Old Testament. For example, in Year 4 when the Old Testament story of Jacob is the main lection, the companion is John 1:50–51. "Jesus answered [Nathanael], 'Do you believe because I told you that I saw you under the fig tree? You will see greater things than these.' And [Jesus] said to him, 'Very truly I tell you, you will see heaven opened and the angels of God ascending and descending upon the Son of [Humanity]." Clearly, as a companion text, these verses allude to the story of Jacob's ladder as well as a transformation of the image—Jesus himself is the ladder in the New Testament.[34] Furthermore,

---

33 My own congregation included these shorter readings each Sunday in the fall and invited some of our younger worshipers to read or recite the passage. Often I intentionally included these Gospel snippets in the middle of my sermon.

34 Prompted by the interplay between the primary and companion text for this Sunday, our congregation projected visual arts related to Jacob's dream and the iconic ladder

a few months later in Year 4, when John 1:35–51 is the main reading, the Old Testament allusion is likely more accessible for folks who have been following the arc of the Narrative Lectionary.

2. Scripture-reading Communities

While many congregations experimenting with the Narrative Lectionary used these scriptures exclusively for Sunday morning worship, others found a variety of ways to enhance their congregation's engagement with the big Story of scripture throughout the week. Weekly Bible studies on the upcoming Sunday's story were typical. One pastor explained that for her Bible study "everyone listened to the Bibleworm Podcast on the Narrative Lectionary scripture in advance. [The podcast] is not too overwhelming in terms of scholarship. It's chatty. And having a Jewish rabbi and a Christian pastor on this podcast is a good check for supersessionist readings." One pastor who occasionally leads morning prayer, evening prayer, or leadership team retreats uses the Narrative Lectionary texts in a practice of "dwelling in the Word" during these gatherings. Another pastor who leads a monthly "stories with seniors" gathering, always includes the upcoming Sunday's scripture: "I say that once a month they write my sermon for me! We just discuss the Bible story and relate it to our lives." This same pastor said, "What's been really significant for me and our congregation is that we've begun telling the scripture [rather than reading it]. Now I never preach without memorizing the story, even if I'm not the one telling it in worship. That way I'm preaching from something I've taken in. This is for our congregation and my own spiritual formation and practice."[35]

Another resource developed for use with the Narrative Lectionary is a schedule of daily readings. One pastor explained that her congregation distributes these daily readings along with a question for family conversation. As a result, some of their families have begun reading the Bible together at home.

Koester, who originally developed the lectionary in his own congregational adult teaching setting and then tested it with other congregations and in seminary courses, emphasizes that music, contemporary and ancient artwork, maps, drama, and nontraditional sermon structures can all enhance our appropriation of the Narrative Lectionary. Most pastors I interviewed became animated as they shared about creative connections to the biblical story that were part of their Narrative Lectionary experience. For example: "We had very cool visuals by a sculpture artist in our congregation who created installations for each Sunday. I especially remember the one from Genesis and the creation stories."

---

full of angels, as well as a ladder-like DNA spiral, acknowledging Jesus as the incarnate divine Word.

35 This pastor's practice of telling scriptures has emerged from work with the Network of Biblical Storytellers International referenced earlier.

Another pastor whose congregation had the habit of a sermon discussion class, even before their Narrative Lectionary experience, said, "We have a weekly discussion group (after worship) based on the sermon. This is an Anabaptist way of thinking about the sermon and engaging multiple voices."[36]

In my own congregation I've frequently projected global Christian artwork related to the scripture of the day. This has contributed to decolonizing our images of biblical characters (and interpretations), engaging our aesthetic sensibilities, and connecting us to other Christian communities around the world and across the centuries. As Meghan Larissa Good puts it, "The Bible trains our eye for the divine aesthetic and then sends us out with a brush in hand to paint with the help of the Master."[37]

3. Self-Disciplined Leadership

A number of pastors spoke about how the Narrative Lectionary broadened their selection of scripture texts for preaching:

- One pastor admitted she avoided preaching from the Epistles when using the RCL because she always had a choice. For her, the Narrative Lectionary's inclusion of New Testament letters to the early churches has proved to be a good corrective in the post-Easter season.
- Another pastor observed that "the danger in preaching, as an Anabaptist (or any other confessional tradition), is to sit with what I want to preach. We're not the only Christians on the planet. Our Anabaptist emphases are important, but the Narrative Lectionary helps us tell the whole story. We're a justice-minded, justice-oriented congregation, but we are sometimes too issue-oriented and this lectionary takes us into the narrative, the personal stories of people with God."
- A pastor who recognized both the Anabaptist focus on a Christ-centered gospel of peace and the need for recognizing this theme through the biblical canon said, "Peace/Shalom is God's intention from the beginning of the biblical narrative, and it's foundational to how we understand God. Jesus wasn't sent to bring a new idea."

---

36 In *Fire by Night*, Florer-Bixler links this "Anabaptist way" to earlier church practices. When church members were frustrated by the challenges of biblical interpretation and wishing for angelic answers, fourth-century African theologian Augustine of Hippo explained to them that "the work of interpretation is not for instruction alone; it is for creating a temple out of God's people, a task that leads us toward love, 'pouring soul into soul'" (from *De doctrina christiana*, Preface 6, 34).

37 Meghan Larissa Good, *The Bible Unwrapped: Making Sense of Scripture Today* (Harrisonburg, VA: Herald, 2018), 43.

- Another wise pastor said, "I like structure, so rather than creating my own, I like a system that has me preaching texts I may not have chosen on my own."

4. Minding the Gaps

The Narrative Lectionary doesn't include every Bible story—sorry, Samson!—and it doesn't include every story in its entirety. However, Koester explains that the Narrative Lectionary does give the Old Testament a more coherent voice than many congregations have experienced before.

Given that the Old Testament is much longer than the New Testament and that the Narrative Lectionary focuses on a Gospel from Christmas to Easter, the Old Testament lections in the fall cover a lot of ground in a few months. To tell the big Story well, some pastors are creatively bridging the gap between one story and the next. For example, one pastor created a fall Bible study series that dovetailed with the Narrative Lectionary's sweep through the Old Testament, adding even more stories and context. Some congregations distributed the daily Narrative Lectionary passages, which also fill in the gaps in the big Story of scripture. Others found that the Narrative Lectionary increased their opportunity for teaching, and they projected or printed visuals and timelines for their congregations, especially during the Old Testament stories.

Pastors also intentionally bridged gaps in the Gospel readings. When the focus was on Luke, for instance, one pastor prepared short virtual teaching sessions on key themes in the Gospel such as wealth/poverty. Another congregation tried to "build a bridge" between one story and the next during the opening of the worship service each week or during their children's time in worship. Another pastor oriented her congregation by projecting a Bible timeline each Sunday with an arrow indicating "You are here." With my own congregation, I have included short comments (written and video) in our digital newsletter to illustrate the relationships between lections from one week to the next as well as the relationships between these parts of scripture and our context for mission.

Formation and Witness Reflections: Words of Appreciation from the Pastors

While I certainly felt blessed to hear from these gifted pastors, in the course of the interviews I also heard their appreciation for the opportunity I was providing them to review their preaching/teaching ministries in light of formation and witness needs in their contexts:

- One pastor who graduated from seminary decades ago had recently begun reading more feminist, BIPOC, and queer theology. He said, "In our context the Narrative Lectionary makes sense because story is fluid, not propositional. Story opens up space. I think the Narrative Lectionary has helped us handle sacred texts in a more holistic way . . . as story. Story invites us into a journey—intellectually, emotionally, spiritually, and psychologically. Theology becomes an active practice, not static."

- A pastor in his first decade of formal ministry, reflecting on the labor of congregational formation in the biblical story, said, "Scripture reveals that there are miraculous moments that occur, but these seem to be brief windows. There is also a lot of time when communities are preparing and waiting in the meantime. For example—Pentecost. The apostles didn't seek it out. Pentecost happened to them. Perhaps the waiting is a significant part of the ministry calling. I need to preach with the awareness that the church is usually non-dynamic, but preach so that when the Spirit comes, she comes here . . . because we were waiting and ready."
- Another pastor who enjoyed her first year preaching from the Narrative Lectionary reported, "I found the scriptures speaking so directly to what was happening in our world—especially racism, violence, and political dysfunction. I personally find it comforting to realize that even given the troubles of our time and national context we didn't invent oppression, or dominating power; it's part of human history and shows up in the biblical story."
- Reflecting on our Anabaptist-minded context for ministry, one pastor said she believes the Narrative Lectionary "may be more conducive to communal interpretation of scripture because congregational members are stepping into the same stream of the biblical story—even if they miss a Sunday or two."
- Another pastor explained, "For me the Bible is the story of God's people, and the Narrative Lectionary allows people to experience that. It connects the Old Testament and New Testament and fits the way I think about the Bible."
- Another leader identified herself primarily as a disciple, a learner, when she said, "As a pastor, being deeply engaged with the Narrative Lectionary scriptures across all the age groups I work with keeps me learning myself. I want to keep getting excited about the Bible."

Concluding Queries

I conclude with several directions for future queries—my own and perhaps yours:

- The Lutheran gift to the ecumenical community in the form of a Narrative Lectionary and related curricula is a blessing to Mennonite leaders seeking to form congregations for witness through the biblical story. What might this cycle of scripture readings stir in your congregation?
- While the Narrative Lectionary has only been around for about a decade

and is still an experiment, certainly so for Mennonite congregations, I invite other Anabaptist-minded Christian formation leaders to join the experiment by using the Narrative Lectionary and then reflecting on the congregational outcomes with respect to our capacity for witness. Have we a story to tell?

- I recommend that Mennonites, at both the congregational and denominational level, begin to link the scriptures we use for worship/preaching with the scriptures we use in other curriculum-based Christian formation contexts. Might sharing the same biblical story intergenerationally week to week suggest that we indeed share a common Story generation to generation? That adults need the queries and engagement of children/youth and vice versa in order to better engage our local contexts as God's people?
- Finally, I shared a few tears with the pastor who asked, "There are many places where we can look for the sacred story. There are so many people craving the liberating word. Where does that magic happen? If some don't experience the balm of hearing scripture, as I do, what do we offer?" As if in partial response to her own question, and like Jesus, himself known for answering a question with a question when it seemed best, she then asked, "What are we doing together as a body to create experiences of the gospel?"

In a 2021 keynote address to the Network of Biblical Storytellers International, Richard Ward said, "Having trouble with the text? Welcome to the family!" Ward went on to clarify that our congregations are not so much biblically illiterate as "tone deaf to the sacred story. We doubt both the Bible's capacity to speak to life today and the ordinary Christian's capacity to interpret scripture well." He recommends that in times like this we learn to live with the Bible as we would with a companion.

Taking a cue from Ward, I am attracted to the metaphor of friendship to describe our relationship with the Bible.[38] In light of today's digital age, perhaps the Narrative Lectionary may be likened to an app connecting congregations to their sacred story and facilitating friendship across great distances. As we teach

38 Jeff Barker describes an experience of a group of college students presenting Old Testament scriptures from memory: "Suddenly an ancient power was in the room. It was a reunion with an old friend who had been hidden by cold readings. We were once again remembering the beauty of the story of God." See Jeff Barker, "Scripture and the Arts of Story, Movement, and Music," in *Worship and Mission for the Global Church: An Ethnodoxology Handbook*, ed. James R. Krabill (Pasadena, CA: William Carey Library, 2013), 468.

and preach from the whole Bible, Christian formation leaders foster a companionable relationship of trust between our congregations and the biblical story. And the Author, whose signature posture is to not sit over us but dwell beside us and stir within us, delights to call us friends.

Narrative Lectionary (NL) Resources:

Text Studies & Worship Resources

https://www.workingpreacher.org/narrative-faq

- Basic orientation to the Narrative Lectionary, including the summer modules created so far, and commentary.

https://www.workingpreacher.org/home-narrative-lectionary

Worship resources linked to the NL

https://clergystuff.com/

- Worship and other congregational resources linked to the NL (some free and some for purchase) by Kace Leetch (kace@clergystuff.com).

http://www.textweek.com/

- Originally designed for RCL, this site now also links to NL resources.

Christian Formation Curriculum and Ministry with Children

https://spiritandtruthpublishing.com/

- Published by Gregory Dawn. Some Mennonite congregations have used these Christian faith formation resources as their Sunday school curriculum for children and youth.

https://www.spillthebeans.org.uk/

- Published by the Church of Scotland, this resource includes four years of NL commentary as well as education, worship, and music resources.

https://storypath.upsem.edu/

- This resource from Union Presbyterian Seminary connects a children's storybook to themes from the NL each week.

Music

https://wordtoworship.com/lectionary/narrative?year=2021

- Includes many contemporary worship songs that are linked to NL themes for each week.

Podcasts

https://www.workingpreacher.org/podcasts

- Three Luther Seminary professors, including the two originators of the NL, discuss the week's texts.

https://www.pulpitfiction.com/

- Hosted by a United Church of Christ and a United Methodist pastor. There is now a Narrative Cast podcast.

https://www.biblewormpodcast.com/

- Hosted by two Bible scholars—one Christian and one Jewish: Amy Robertson and Robert Williamson, Jr. Focuses on NL texts.

Blogs

- https://storied.org/lectionary/
- https://revgalblogpals.org/category/narrative-lectionary/

Other Resources

Several pastors mentioned resources that were not explicitly linked to the NL but worked well with the broader concept of teaching the whole biblical story:

- https://www.hesston.edu/academics/departments/bible-and-ministry/timeline/
- Heilsgeschichte Timeline developed at Hesston (Kansas) College
- Sally Lloyd-Jones, *The Jesus Storybook Bible: Every Story Whispers His Name* (Grand Rapids, MI: Zonderkidz, 2017).
- https://bibleproject.com/
  These short 6–8 minute videos, especially the biblical book overviews, are useful in teaching settings.

Book Reviews

Katharine Hayhoe, *Saving Us: A Climate Scientist's Case for Hope and Healing in a Divided World*, Atria/One Signal, New York, 2021. 320 pp. $22.99. ISBN-13: 978-1982143855.

Katherine Hayhoe is a climate scientist, an evangelical Christian, a long-term Texas resident, and a brilliant communicator. In *Saving Us*, she doesn't say anything that can't be found elsewhere, but she says it so well that this book is a must-read for anyone seeking constructive and effective ways to address climate change.

Hayhoe covers a lot of the ground you would expect to read about: the reality of the climate crisis, its impacts, the technologies and policies that can make a difference. But this book's importance lies elsewhere—in helping us navigate the challenges of communicating with each other about this fraught topic.

Most readers of this review will be familiar with the tension between commitment to truth and commitment to relationship. Sometimes we must tell people truths that they don't want to hear or just can't hear. (And sometimes people need to give us messages that we don't want to hear.) While there is something fundamentally wrong about building relationships that depend on the assumption of untruths, sometimes the truth appears to get in the way of opportunities for meaningful relationship.

For multiple reasons—political polarization, false narratives in popular media, reluctance to face fears—this tension is particularly acute when it comes to the findings of climate science. And this is where Hayhoe is most helpful.

In the chapter "The Problem with Facts," she says:

> Basing our opinions and judgments on reason rather than emotion is the lofty goal laid out by Greek philosophers. It continues to be pursued by scientists today. But Plato might be disappointed to learn that modern psychology strongly suggests that when it comes to making up our minds about something, emotions usually come first and reason second. If we've already formed our opinions, more information will get filtered through those pre-existing frames. And the more closely that frame is tied to our sense of what makes us a good person, the more tightly we'll cling to it and let potentially opposing facts pass us by. As Jonathan Haidt explains in *The Righteous Mind*, "People made moral judgments quickly and emotionally. . . . We do moral reasoning not to reconstruct the actual reasons why we ourselves came to a judgment;

> we reason to find the best possible reasons why somebody else ought to join us in our judgment." (53–54)

Hayhoe illustrates this motivated reasoning via the response of a farmer at a workshop on how climate change affects agriculture in Texas:

> Everything you said makes sense, and I'd like to agree with you. . . .
> But if I agree with you, I have to agree with Al Gore, and I could never do that. (55)

She continues:

> As Peter Boghossian and James Lindsay explain in *How to Have Impossible Conversations*, "Think of every conversation as being three conversations at once: about facts, feelings, and identity." I thought I was having a conversation about farming and water; but we were also talking about how we felt about climate change, and about how we saw ourselves in relation to it. "It might appear that the conversation is about facts and ideas," these authors continue, "but you're inevitably having a discussion about morality, and that, in turn, is inevitably a discussion about what it means to be a good or bad person." The farmer had listened to what I'd said and given it a fair shot, and he even agreed with it—logically. But he realized that he'd have to give up his moral judgment to accept this new information. It just wasn't worth it. (55–56)

Another example recounts a filmed encounter in which Hayhoe and (former Republican congressman) Bob Inglis tried to convince megachurch pastor Rick Joyner of the validity of the findings of climate science—through argument and through demonstration of impacts on oyster fishermen in a place he knew well. She describes Joyner as

> . . . a smart man. In addition to being the head of a large and successful organisation, he is a pilot who understands weather nearly as well as a local meteorologist. And he's also a Dismissive. . . . All of this meant he was better at motivated reasoning and more likely to be polarized by additional information than the average person, rather than less. And that's exactly what happened.
>
> The more we spoke, the more his rejection hardened. . . . He definitely felt that his identity, not his opinions, were being challenged and judged. Unfortunately, the result was to drive [him] even further away, and today his denial is stronger than ever. The same zombie arguments Bob and I responded to back then continue to be hauled out and re-aired at family gatherings, in group text conversations and phone calls. And it's not entirely his fault, either. It's the way our brains work. (57)

When opinions are polarized, when identities are at stake, it's just very hard to reach people with rational argument.

So how do we then communicate difficult messages? Over several chapters, Hayhoe goes on to show that it is counterproductive to use emotional shortcuts of guilt, fear, and shame. She explains how it can sometimes be appropriate to communicate anxiety or anger but only if at the same time we offer hope. "Sermons on hellfire and damnation are only effective in spurring action if there's a chance, however slim, of redemption and forgiveness" (82).

And she ends up—maybe predictably, but it's worth being reminded—with this:

> So how do we move beyond fear or shame? By acting from love, I believe. Love starts with speaking truth: making people fully aware of the risks and the choices they face in a manner that is relevant and practical to them. But it also offers compassion, understanding, and acceptance: the opposite of guilt and shame. Love bolsters our courage, too: what will we not do for those . . . that we love? And finally, it opens the door to that most ephemeral and sought after of emotions, hope. (83)

We live in a time of global emergency, when our need for both hope and love is intensifying, not least to fuel motivation to address the crisis. Hayhoe offers us important tools for the task.

MARK BIGLAND-PRITCHARD *attends Osler (Saskatchewan) Mennonite Church and serves as Migration & Resettlement Coordinator for MCC Saskatchewan. For years, Mark has been a climate activist in the prairies, a context where conversations around global warming and the need for a new economy are largely resisted, requiring much love and courage.*

Review Essay

Mark Jantzen and John D. Thiesen, eds., *European Mennonites and the Holocaust*, University of Toronto Press, Toronto, 2021. 337 pp. $39.95 CND (paperback). ISBN-13: 978-1487525545.

In 2015, in my capacity as a member of the executive board of Mennonite Church USA, I was the chair of the Resolutions Committee for the July delegate assembly in Kansas City. Earlier that year, months before our national convention, I got a call from an unidentified number. "Hello, this is Isaac," I answered. Without warning, the person on the line began to lambast me for allowing, in my role as chair, a resolution to be scheduled for presentation to the delegates that included our acknowledgment of Christian antisemitism. The person quoted a line from the church document that the delegates would be considering in the summer: "We acknowledge the need for repentance of our own complicity in the history of violence committed by Christians against Jews." I explained that my committee had determined that the resolution met all of the requirements, and that our executive board had approved the language of the paragraph in question as appropriate for consideration by the delegate body. Confidently, the man told me that Mennonites were not complicit in anti-Jewish violence and certainly did not play a role in the Nazi atrocities of World War II—*alleged* atrocities, he added.

Shocked and bewildered by his claim, I tried to argue that Christians in the West haven't finished reckoning with the complicity of our traditions in the Holocaust, that our ancestors in the faith failed in their solidarity with Jews, and that we need to remain vigilant in how Christian anti-Judaism sneaks its way into our theologies. "You don't know what you're talking about," he cut me off. "You're not even a real Mennonite. You're not from our people." Then he hung up.

Over the past twenty years as a member of the Mennonite church, I've discovered that my ecclesial siblings who are able to trace their lineage from a long line of Mennonite descendants are always having to engage in the complicated work of sorting through the relationship between their ethnicity and their faith, their biological genealogy and their church commitments. For them, the one has everything to do with the other, which means the inclusion of people like me involves a double-take at their own sense of belonging, a rethinking of what they mean when they claim a Mennonite identity. Are they Mennonite because of their baptism, their church membership? Or are they Mennonite because of the plight of their great-grandparents? Perhaps a little of both?

For most Mennonites, my claim to membership in the Mennonite tradition is welcomed as good news, as an affirmation of the faithfulness of their biological ancestors. For them, my existence as a non-ethnic Mennonite is a sign of a healthy tradition, evidence of a Christian people capacious enough to include believers beyond the ethnic family. For others, however, like the man on the phone, my presence in the church—further, my leadership position—pushes them beyond the limits of their tolerance, which leads to their entrenchment in a church identity that is also a racial identity. My Mennoniteness doesn't extend down far enough, certainly not into my bloodline, especially since my biological family comes from an other-than-European land: I am of a foreign blood and soil, according to the caller.

The recent historiographic turn to consider Mennonite complicity with the horrors of the Nazi regime in twentieth-century Europe drops us into the heart of these negotiations of identity. Mark Jantzen and John Thiesen's edited volume, *European Mennonites and the Holocaust*, invites us into important conversations not only about Mennonite culpability but also Mennonite identity. On the one hand, this is the book I can now recommend to Mennonite Holocaust deniers. I've met one such man, and I imagine there might be others. On the other hand, as a non-European Mennonite, I wonder how the authors in this collection consider my identity as implicated in their narratives.

The argument of the book, as a whole, is for (ethnic?) Mennonites to come to terms with their (our?) involvement in the Holocaust. The editors make the ethical import clear with the Bible passages they chose as epigraphs: "When you offer many prayers, I am not listening," they offer, citing God's condemnation from the first chapter of Isaiah. "Your hands are full of blood!" They also include the words of judgment from Jesus's parable of the sheep and the goats in Matthew 25: "Then he will say to those on his left, 'Depart from me, you who are cursed, into the eternal fire prepared for the devil and his angels.'" In their introduction, the editors comment on their selection of these passages to frame the book: "The biblical epigrams at the beginning of this book refer to Mennonites who collectively have blood on their hands but cannot fit that image into their self-understanding." They shift pronouns from "their" in this sentence to "we" in the next. "We see ourselves as sheep doing good in the name of Christ, not as goats deserving judgment" (18). These subtle shifts in subjectivity occur throughout the book without attention to the complications of representation regarding who speaks on behalf of whom, as well as the complexities of claiming an other's moral obligation to receive such storytelling as an articulation of their own identity.

Those complexities aside (I will return to them later), the violences documented in the book are horrific. The authors recount stories of people who participated in the Nazi genocide, as well as stories of people who looked away while communities of Jews were displaced and massacred. The histories retold in these pages range from active complicity to passive benefit. As a reader, the book unnerved me—the accounts of the way that racial violence takes hold of an entire society and the ease in which the nonresistant could remain quiet in the land while their neighbors disappeared.

A haunting site, around which three chapters revolve, is the district of Zaporizhzhia in what is now Ukraine, where, upon Hitler's seizure of the region, his soldiers methodically eradicated the Jewish population. "In total, in the Zaporizhia region, more than 14,000 Jews and 10,000 POWs and around 600 Roma were murdered," Dmytro Myeshkov writes in chapter 7. "When the city of Zaporizhia was occupied by the Germans in October 1941, the Jewish population numbered 1,841 persons. By spring 1942," he continues, "they had all been murdered" (210). That same spring, across the river from the mass executions, the beleaguered remnants of the historic Mennonite settlement in Khortytsya, now liberated from Soviet repression, gathered for an Easter service—their first in a decade, Aileen Friesen recounts in chapter 8. "Even though the [Jewish] massacre did not happen close to the church," she writes, "it is not hard to imagine that rumours about this event drifted to the Khortytsya side of the Dnieper River" (230).

I followed one of Friesen's endnotes to a 2015 interview with a survivor of the Zaporizhzhia massacre. In the video, Leonid Lerner recounts the gruesome cruelty of that day—March 28, 1942, he remembers, the first day of Passover. "In spite of everything," he says, "the Jews were preparing to celebrate Pesach." German soldiers went door-to-door, interrupting the holiness of the day, and forced Jews to march to the outskirts of the city where they were lined up on a hill and ordered to take off their clothes. Lerner says he can't forget his little brother's face when a soldier pierced through him with a bayonet. "And I still remember his eyes."[1]

Each number added to the millions of killings during the Holocaust points to an unimaginable terror—one atrocity sloughed upon another, mounds of death. "A statistical compilation of those slaughtered in a pogrom," Horkheimer and Adorno wrote in 1944, "conceals its essence, which emerges only in an exact description of the exception, the most hideous torture."[2] *European Mennonites and the Holocaust* reaches through the numbers into the events, into the lives of the perpetrators of violence, into their communities. The book attempts to describe the hideousness of history.

The tension within the book has to do with whether the individuals who were complicit in the atrocities were Mennonites—and, relatedly, if their identity as Mennonites implicates those of us who claim Mennonite identity today. To stick with the chapters on Zaporizhzhia for a moment, Myeshkov pinpoints the obscurities involved in incriminating a perpetrator's identity in the act of violence:

> In each case one must ask which characteristic or bundle of characteristics is decisive or sufficient for identifying this or that person as a Mennonite. The profound changes that took place in the Mennonite community in Ukraine and Crimea as a result of social upheavals during this era only make the task more daunting. Violent modernization accelerated the changes in Mennonite identity and exacerbated the generational conflict that was already developing in the early twentieth century. (218)

Some aspects of the past are more knowable than others. Historians make the best of the available archives in their attempts to capture a person's iden-

---

1 University of Southern California Shoah Foundation, "Shooting of the Jewry of Zaporozhye in the Sovkhoz Named after Stalin in March, 1942" March 1, 2022. I accessed the interview through the online collection of the Babyn Yar Holocaust Memorial Center, https://babynyar.org/en/library/collection/36/5186.

Note: The Ukrainian city and region commonly rendered in English as Zaporizhzhia can also be spelled (as evident elsewhere in the review) as Zaporizhia or Zaporozhye (the latter a transliteration of the Russian spelling).

2 Max Horkheimer and Theodor W. Adorno, *Dialectic of Enlightenment: Philosophical Fragments*, trans. Edmund Jephcott (Stanford, CA: Stanford University Press, 2002), 92–93.

tity. Myeshkov is honest about the difficulties involved in positing a person's Mennoniteness. In Friesen's chapter, she locates in the archives a self-identified Mennonite resident of Zaporizhzhia who joined the *Sicherheitsdienst*, the Nazi secret service, as an intelligence officer—Jacob Fast who "listed his religion as 'Mennonite,'" according to the German immigration and naturalization office (238). Friesen carefully documents how a person identifies their Mennonite identity. At the end of her chapter, however, she gestures toward the widespread involvement of Mennonites as informants who cooperated with the German forces, noting that after the German defeat, under Soviet interrogation, Nazi soldiers and agents named local collaborators who had "Mennonite" surnames—"men with Mennonite last names," Friesen writes, who were "intimately involved in the violence perpetrated during the occupation" (241). In this case a surname was enough, according to Friesen, to imply Mennonite identity.

In their description of the criteria for who counts as a Mennonite, the editors outline "overlapping possibilities" of identity, which includes the status of a person's genealogy. "A simplistic approach is to assume that a Mennonite is someone with a 'Mennonite name' who comes from a 'Mennonite family'" (12); "A cultural approach casts a wide enough net to include those whose grandparents and parents were Mennonite, even if the person in question never entered a Mennonite church" (14). Doris L. Bergen, in her brief introduction to Gerhard Rempel's chapter, provides a full-throated defense of this biological approach to Mennonite identity. "It is second nature and a kind of game to spot 'Mennonite names,'" Bergen writes about her experience of growing up in a Euroethnic Mennonite community. This method "implies a practical approach that, in my assessment, turns out to be the most historically sound way to deal with the challenge of defining who counts as a Mennonite for purposes of studying 'Mennonites and the Holocaust'" (38).[3] This *most historically sound* approach, which Bergen notes as a kind of game that Euroethnic Mennonites play with each other, occurs throughout the book. The irony, of course, is that this method of determining Mennonite identity mimics the Nazi racial logic of peoplehood—"the importance of the biological background of existence," as Horst Quiring, a Mennonite minister and theologian in Berlin, lauded the Nazi commitment to the "mightiness of the blood" (131).[4]

---

3 Here is one example among many in Gerhard Rempel's chapter, "Mennonites, War Crimes, and the Holocaust," where he considers a person's blood relations as enough to identify the individual as a Mennonite: "An atrocity had been committed by the son of Mennonites near the former Mennonite settlements of Templehof, Suvorovka, Olgino, and Terek" (62).

4 Several authors in the volume point to the theological contributions of Horst Quiring, a Mennonite pastor with Nazi sympathies, as an influential voice—beginning with his 1938 book *Grundworte des Glaubens*—in articulating a Euroethnic Mennonite identi-

In chapter 2, James Irvin Lichti writes about the sinister complicity of this so-called "Mennonite game" with Nazi ideologies of nativism:

> The seemingly innocuous habits of genealogy and "the Mennonite game" dovetailed all too tidily with these racial notions: a susceptibility to Nazi racial ideology ran through German Mennonite congregations and surfaced even in periodical content. Nazi propagandists used this racialized version of Mennonite history to their own ends, promoting the "racial purity" of Mennonite communities throughout the world in racial periodicals, popular novels, and a feature-length studio movie. (88)

Blood kinship as Mennonite belonging proved admirable to German racial anthropologists. This likeness troubles Litchti, who seems to worry about the perpetuation of conceptions of Mennonite identity that correlate to *Völkisch* constructions of peoplehood.[5]

I acknowledge that my own Mennonite identity is ecclesial; while Hinojosa and Francisco surnames are familiar to me, I don't know anybody named Jantzen or Wiens. My Mennoniteness has everything to do with the relationships I've formed according to congregational membership. Strangely, the editors of this volume do not include this as one of their many criteria for a person's identification as a Mennonite. (The category they call "theological identity" has to do with the subjectivity of belief rather than the objectivity of baptism and church membership—see pages 12–17.) Despite the editors' omission of this identity, several of the authors demonstrate their careful research in determining whether a person was baptized or joined a Mennonite church. For example, this concern is central to Alle G. Hoekema's chapter on Dutch Mennonites.[6]

---

ty in alignment with Nazi formulations of racial purity. "What it means to be a people has only recently become clear," Imanuel Baumann quotes from Quiring's book. "A people is not formed by a commonality in land, language, or history, but has its deepest foundation in the community of blood or race" (111).

5 For a helpful account of Nazi constructions of racial identities, see Claudia Koonz, *The Nazi Conscience* (Cambridge, MA: The Belknap Press of the Harvard University Press, 2003), especially chapters 5 ("Ethnic Revival and Racist Anxiety") and 8 ("The Quest for a Respectable Racism").

6 Hoekema, in "Dutch Mennonites and Yad Vashem Recognition," includes the story of the van Drooge family, whose father, Alexander, was a Mennonite pastor. Residents of the Dutch village of Makkum, the family was involved in the underground resistance efforts against Nazi occupation and participated in clandestine operations to hide Jews and assist in their escape. I hadn't known of this Mennonite family that had tried to convince the parents of Etty Hillesum to hide their family in the Mennonite parsonage. (When they were youth, the van Drooge parents had been students at the high school where Dr. Louis Hillesum, Etty's father, was the director.) To read the accounts in this book—like this one about the Hillesum family—is to be entangled in the endless looping of history's

This is not to discount the storytelling and historical research documented in the book. The "Mennonite game" approach to historiography investigates a person's situatedness in a familial clan, and many of the authors of these chapters engage in the intimate work of revisiting uncomfortable truths about their own family stories. "Many of the scholars in this volume have a personal involvement with their subjects," the editors disclose, "though not all have chosen to discuss those ties" (19). For these reasons the book is courageous. The authors offer us a profound gift in their remarkable bravery—confession of their progenitors' complicity in what was done and left undone, to interrupt the repression of legacies of harm that take hold of our lives.

In chapter 6, for instance, Colin P. Neufeldt recounts his grandparents' (and their community's) willingness to benefit from the Nazi occupation in Poland: "These Mennonites had witnessed Nazi brutality toward the Jews, yet they chose to continue working for the Nazi authorities" (184). In chapter 11, Hans Werner notes his father's military involvement: "My father fought as a solider both for the Red Army and for the Wehrmacht (the regular German Army)" (294). In the concluding chapter, Steven Schroeder wrestles with his heritage as a descendent of Mennonites from the Danzig area who engaged in military duties: "My grandfather and many other relatives served in the German military, and I remember the portraits of them in Wehrmacht uniforms that hung on my grandparents' walls" (308).

To narrate these violences is courageous work, an example for all of us who have not had the fortitude to unfold our family stories, to lay out an unflinching account of the iniquities of ancestors in order to enable repentance. Schroeder ends his chapter with an invitation for other Mennonites to join his family's Mennonite identity, to engage in an ethics of atonement: "Regardless of our respective religious views and practices, our cultural affinity to Mennonitism, or our last names, this is our heritage—a heritage that impacts our personhood, our engagement with the people around us, and the broader world" (315). This is quite the assumption, in terms of speaking for anyone and everyone who considers themselves Mennonite—as if Schroeder's genealogy subsumes mine, as if I am required to find a place in his family tree in order to belong in the Mennonite story. A generous interpretation would involve a decision to hear in his declaration, despite the colonial overtones, a petition for others to bear the burden of his heritage with him, to take his assertion as a plea for solidarity—his cry as an appeal for companions so that he would not have to suffer alone the guilt he feels for his family's history.

As a Mennonite without any bloodline connections to Euroethnic Mennonites, my avenue into these horrors has been my belonging within Western

---

"what ifs," the unnerving hope for alternate endings to undo the tragic, to wish for the slightest of changes that would have made all the difference in the world.

Christianity. I am part of a faith that facilitated the rise of the Nazi regime. The following studies over the past several decades have proven fundamental for me in understanding the sinister complicities of European Christianity in Nazism: Robert P. Erickson's *Theologians under Hitler: Gerhard Kittel, Paul Althaus, and Emanuel Hirsch*; Doris L. Bergen's *Twisted Cross: The German Christian Movement in the Third Reich*; and Susannah Heschel's *The Aryan Jesus: Christian Theologians and the Bible in Nazi Germany*.[7]

As I read *European Mennonites and the Holocaust*, I thought a lot about the current religious and political situation here in the United States as evangelical Christianity has become synonymous with the quasi-fascist politics of the Trumpian movement. As a Pew Research Center study revealed last year, the election of President Trump resulted in more US citizens declaring themselves evangelical; his political campaign served as a missional event for evangelicalism, his rallies as evangelical revivals.[8] We've been warned about such ominous possibilities; we've had prophets—for example, George Jackson's dispatches from prison ("the U.S. as a fascist-corporative state")[9] and Sheldon Wolin's discernment regarding the fascist transformation of the US political project into "Superpower Democracy," "Inverted Totalitarianism."[10] Dorothee Sölle, was perhaps the most prescient in linking the Christianity of Nazi Germany to evangelicalism in the United States when she coined the term "Christofascism" to describe the situation on this side of the Atlantic, where a particular theological culture has produced a faith befitting those who crave political dominance.[11]

European Mennonites and the Holocaust certainly offers a caution to ethnically European Mennonites whose ancestors were all too willing to recognize their

---

7 Robert P. Erickson, *Theologians under Hitler: Gerhard Kittel, Paul Althaus, and Emanuel Hirsch* (New Haven, CT: Yale University Press, 1987); Doris L. Bergen, *Twisted Cross: The German Christian Movement in the Third Reich* (Chapel Hill, NC: University of North Carolina Press, 1996); Susannah Heschel, *The Aryan Jesus: Christian Theologians and the Bible in Nazi Germany* (Princeton, NJ: Princeton University Press, 2008).

8 Gregory Smith, "More White Americans Adopted than Shed Evangelical Label During Trump Presidency, Especially His Supporters," September 15, 2021, Pew Research Center, https://www.pewresearch.org/fact-tank/2021/09/15/more-white-americans-adopted-than-shed-evangelical-label-during-trump-presidency-especially-his-supporters/.

9 George L. Jackson, *Blood in My Eye* (Baltimore, MD: Black Classic, 1990), 134.

10 Sheldon S. Wolin, *Democracy Incorporated: Managed Democracy and the Specter of Inverted Totalitarianism* (Princeton, NJ: Princeton University Press, 2008).

11 Dorothee Sölle, "Christofascism," *The Window of Vulnerability: A Political Spirituality, trans. Linda M. Maloney* (Minneapolis, MN: Fortress, 1990), 133–41. William E. Connolly, who does not seem to be aware of Sölle's work, provides a more recent account of the effect of evangelicalism upon the US political situation in *Capitalism and Christianity, American Style* (Durham, NC: Duke University Press, 2008).

Mennonite identity as a racial identity in order to take advantage of a hierarchically racialized social order. That historical realization, I imagine, has affected the consciousness of their descendants who now benefit from their whiteness while making a home in the settler colonial regimes of North America. I had hoped to find more in these chapters that would extend these important issues beyond consciousness-raising work for those who are able to locate themselves in the European Mennonite family tree.

One place in the book that can spur a conversation—beyond the quasi-ethnic studies approach to the Mennonite tradition—occurs at the end of Arnold Neufeldt-Fast's chapter on German Mennonite theology, where he hints at a diagnosis of a theological problem still operational in our churches—that is, a penchant for theologies of victory instead of theologies that cultivate a disposition of vulnerability. "Theologically, there has been a growing consensus," Neufeldt-Fast writes, "that all *Christian* talk of God requires reference to God's own Trinitarian self-definition in weakness and death for the sake of life" (140).[12] This observation resounds with Johann Baptist Metz's summons in 1981 for Christians in the West to put the brakes on triumphalist doctrines of victoriousness.[13] "Christianity victoriously conceals its own messianic weakness," he observed. "Does there not exist something like a typically Christian incapacity for dismay in the face of disasters?"[14] Metz warned against a | distinctly progressive Christian preference for theological narratives of victory, and instead encouraged conceptions of messianic weakness that would render our theologies vulnerable to tragedy, a posture open to the undoing of the self-assured coherence of theological narratives of victory—the undoing of narratives that confirm our own sense that we are on the right side of history, that we are always on God's side and never in a position to be numbered among the enemies of God.[15] Perhaps this direction of concern should lead us to re-exam-

---

12 Neufeldt-Fast points to Jürgen Moltmann's *The Crucified God* for this line of exploration. I think Moltmann's proposals end up instigating more problems than they solve in terms of the intra-Trinitarian relations (i.e., God *in se*). Alan Lewis explains the achievements and shortcomings of Moltmann's theological project in chapter 7, "From God's Passion to God's Death," of *Between Cross and Resurrection: A Theology of Holy Saturday* (Grand Rapids, MI: Eerdmans, 2001), 197–257.

13 Johann Baptist Metz, "Christians and Jews after Auschwitz," *The Emergent Church: The Future of Christianity in a Postbourgeois World* (New York, NY: Crossroad, 1981), 22.

14 Metz, "Christians and Jews after Auschwitz," 25.

15 The editors note the following tendency among progressive North American Mennonites: "By the twenty-first century, progressive Mennonites [in Canada and the United States] had shifted from rejecting military service as a key component of a collective identity to seeing Mennonites as proponents of peace and justice claims on be-

ine the prevalence of *Christus victor* theologies within North American ecclesial life (especially among US Christian progressives),[16] because such triumphalist theologies locate the faithful on the side of the victor, not on the side of the people in need of repentance and forgiveness.[17] Christian proclamation should also inspire us to confess sins—to acknowledge that, for example, when we read the New Testament gospel narratives as invitations into the Christian life, we often find ourselves with the disciples who betray Jesus.

Isaac S. Villegas *is the pastor of Chapel Hill Mennonite Fellowship in North Carolina (USA) and serves as the president of the North Carolina Council of Churches.*

half of downtrodden minorities; this view encouraged them to understand themselves as a people always on the 'right' side of history" (18). Notice that the editors assume a twenty-first-century Mennonite identity that does not already include "minorities."

16 For example, J. Denny Weaver has characterized his work, *The Nonviolent Atonement*, as an attempt to revive Gustaf Aulén's articulation (in 1930) of a *Christus Victor* theology, which Weaver renders into a theory of Christ's nonviolent atonement. Although he notes some concerns with Aulén's version of the Christus Victor theory, Weaver locates his own approach as a revitalization project: "I argue that a revised form of it commends itself to the twenty-first century" (J. Denny Weaver, *The Nonviolent Atonement* [Grand Rapids, MI: Eerdmans, 2001], 15). Devin Singh has recently pointed out that Weaver's nonviolent atonement model depends on the logic of economic colonialism: "We need to consider the dynamics of economic annexation and colonialism that are modeled in such a narrative" (Devin Singh, *Divine Currency: The Theological Power of Money in the West* [Stanford, CA: Stanford University Press, 2018], 184–85). Also see J. Alexander Sider, "'Who Durst Defy the Omnipotent to Arms?': The Nonviolent Atonement and a Non-Competitive Doctrine of God," in *The Work of Jesus Christ in Anabaptist Perspective: Essays in Honor of J. Denny Weaver*, eds. Alain Epp Weaver and Gerald J. Mast (Telford, PA: Cascadia, 2008), 246–62.

17 For a brief account of the Christus Victor theory of atonement that contextualizes it within social power relations, see James Wm. Mclendon, Jr., *Doctrine: Systematic Theology*, Volume 2 (Nashville, TN: Abingdon, 1994), 199–203. I'm grateful to Jamie Pitts for pointing me to McClendon's astute observations regarding how the meaning of Christus Victor theories shift according to the church's social status—that the significance has everything to do with whether Christianity operates with majoritarian or minoritarian power within society.

David C. Kirkpatrick, *A Gospel for the Poor: Global Social Christianity and the Latin American Evangelical Left*, University of Pennsylvania Press, Philadelphia, Pennsylvania, 2019. 288 pp. $55.00. ISBN-13: 978-0812250947.

David C. Kirkpatrick's *A Gospel for the Poor: Global Social Christianity and the Latin American Evangelical Left* focuses on the history of the Latin American evangelical "left" movement, presenting its background and influence on global Christianity. Several sources that Kirkpatrick resorts to for building his narrative—such as bilingual interviews, unstudied personal papers, and far-flung archival documents—evidence the originality of his work, providing insight into the untold stories of the political drama of the Latinos/as within the leadership of global evangelicalism. Kirkpatrick aims to show that the current social emphasis within American and European evangelicalism arose primarily from the influence of this Latin American movement. As a Latin American who was once part of this evangelical movement, I will concentrate on Kirkpatrick's revised picture of the origins and development of the movement, and conclude with a brief observation about his narrative as a whole.

To situate the Latin American evangelical "left" movement within a global perspective, Kirkpatrick introduces his work by focusing on one of the most important evangelical gatherings of the twentieth century—the International Congress on World Evangelization, which took place in Lausanne, Switzerland, in 1974. This focus on Lausanne allows him to connect the story of the Latin American movement with the story of two of its leaders, Rene Padilla and Samuel Escobar, both of whom had key roles in the congress. After this setting, the first chapter presents the controversial theological elements that Latin American theologians brought to Lausanne, together with the responses from American and British leaders, such as Billy Graham and John Stott. For Kirkpatrick, the presence of Escobar and Padilla on the platform at Lausanne was not only a symbol of the emerging leadership from the Global South but also a symbol of protest. He highlights how both Escobar and Padilla resort to the notion of *misión integral* (integral mission) to criticize the "mutilated Gospel" of the American middle-class evangelicals. This notion is a key theological concept raised by Latin American evangelicals within missional work. Kirkpatrick's account of Padilla's speech at Lausanne explains integral mission as a comprehensive view of Christian salvation, which touches all aspects of life, including the concern for social justice and the ethical demands of discipleship. For Latin American evangelicals, says Kirkpatrick, Lausanne was all about negotiating this "social" Christianity within the very structures of global evangelicalism. In this respect, the result of the congress—that is, the Lausanne Covenant—must be perceived as a political compromise between Latin Americans and the global evangelical movement led by the North.

In chapter 2, Kirkpatrick shows the background and development of the Latin American evangelical movement before Lausanne, claiming that it is a mistake to consider the movement as a mere version of liberation theology. In that respect, he shows the unique way that the sociopolitical context of violence, oppression, and dependency connected with the evangelical experience. Escobar and Padilla, together with Pedro Arana, were leaders of the International Fellowship of Evangelical Students (IFES) in Latin America in the 1960s, which placed them at the heart of the evangelical global movement, permeating their theological reflection and approach to the political climate of Latin America. Kirkpatrick's narrative shows that for Escobar, Padilla, and Arana the imported evangelical understanding of the gospel was not an option because that discourse did not provide an answer to the questions posed by the Latin American context and liberation theology. As an alternative, the movement originated a parallel space for theological reflection to maintain its evangelical identity—that is, *La Fraternidad Teológica Latinoamericana* (FTL), the "Latin American Theological Fraternity/Fellowship."

As chapters 3 and 4 show, the FTL was born as a rejection of North American and British paternalism but without cutting off relationships with those evangelical networks. The FTL pulled global evangelicalism toward social themes without disconnecting from the North Atlantic world. In this respect, Kirkpatrick notes in chapter 5 that the assumed postcolonial narrative for the emergence of the FTL as an independent Latin American evangelical movement must be nuanced by highlighting the missionary sources that shaped the movement, helped in its development, and allowed the global expansion of its ideas. For Kirkpatrick, the origin of the current global "social" Christianity can only be told in a transnational story that involves the mutual influence of evangelicals in the Southern and Northern hemispheres.

For Kirkpatrick, integral mission theology is not a version of liberation theology, and this becomes clear as he pays attention to the evangelical movement's criticisms of the liberationist theological method. However, as chapter 6 shows, there was also a rich ecumenical dialogue between evangelicals and liberationists. The FTL included Protestant theologians inclined toward liberation theology, such as Orlando Costas and José Míguez Bonino, although the dialogue was more at an interpersonal level than an organizational one. Kirkpatrick says that the dialogue with ecumenical theologians helped widen the purview not only for the Latin American evangelical movement but also for the global evangelical movement, which made room for the inclusion of a "social" evangelicalism. However, as he explains in chapter 7, integral mission theology was later appropriated by international NGOs as a depoliticized synthesis of "pursuing justice and offering salvation" (142), although many missiologists are still challenging the political conservatism within global evangelicalism by resorting to the theological legacy of Latin Americans.

In *A Gospel for the Poor*, Kirkpatrick states that his goal is to offer not only a descriptive story of the Latin American evangelical movement but also a prescriptive narrative that demands for others to recognize the importance of Latinos/as within evangelicalism. In this respect, there are many details in Kirkpatrick's narrative that could be taken as prescriptive elements for the presence of Latinos/as within global evangelical Christianity. Here I will consider three elements: (1) the multidirectional conversation within evangelicalism, (2) the importance of personal relationships, and (3) the theological alternative that Latin Americans represented for global evangelicalism.

First, throughout his narrative, Kirkpatrick attends to the connections between the Latin American and North Atlantic evangelicals, highlighting that these movements were part of a multidirectional conversation within global evangelicalism. In that sense, global evangelicalism should not underestimate Latino/a's contributions. In the same way, it is important to remember that Latinos/as have received multiple benefits from the North besides financial support—for example, the profusion of theological conversation partners that shaped the development of Latin American missional theology. The dangers of neo-colonialism did not deter the dialogues that created the possibility for interdependency, which has produced the present movement of critical global evangelical Christianity.

Next, Kirkpatrick's account centers on the lives of the people who have shaped this movement through their persistent conversations. These relationships have overcome many organizational and institutional divisions. In this respect, it is imperative to recognize the value of friendship within global evangelicalism, and the political skills of leaders who brought together different organizations and institutions for common goals.

And finally, a third important element in Kirkpatrick's work is the claim that the Latin American evangelical movement produced not a different version of liberation theology but an evangelical alternative to it. However, as Kirkpatrick's narrative also shows, it is possible to call into question the movement's own evangelical identity. Latin American theologians recognized early on the troubling theological issues within their evangelical tradition and therefore pushed global evangelicalism toward an alternative. In this respect, the connections with Anàbaptists that Kirkpatrick highlights—such as John Howard Yoder's involvement with the FTL and the "Radical discipleship group," the presence of Anabaptist Brethren missionaries, and Ron Sider as a conversation partner—subtly influenced the discussions of Latin American theologians. This might explain some of the theological emphases that North American Anabaptists and Latin American evangelicals share in common—for example, a focus on the kingdom of God; the centrality of the church and the biblical narrative rather than other communities and ideologies; and the nature of the gospel and mission as an indivisible union of words and actions.

In sum, *A Gospel for the Poor* provides a good picture of the origins and development of the Latin American evangelical "left" movement, highlighting the importance of the Latinos/as within global evangelical Christianity. However, the foreign origin and target of Kirkpatrick's work—a North American perspective directed to North American and European readers—permeates his narrative. For example, Kirkpatrick's use of the designation "left" is hardly neutral. He explicitly states that this designation avoids a blanket categorization of the movement, since many Latin American evangelicals rejected *misión integral*, underscoring that "the emerging coalition of the Latin American Evangelical Left refers primarily to a political orientation rather a theological one—theologically conservative and evangelical while pushing boundaries on socially progressive ideas" (13). Yet, Escobar, Padilla, and the FTL never assumed a partisan perspective nor intended to bring a partisan ideology to global evangelicalism. This Latin American movement consisted of theologians and pastors who were trying to respond to their social and political context with their own understanding of the gospel and with a theological discourse that had political consequences but that could not be subsumed under a political category. In that respect, the main goal of the movement was not to influence the political discourse of global evangelicalism but to change the missional practices that the evangelical theological discourse originated. Therefore, the global impact of this Latin American evangelical movement could be better evaluated not by assessing its influence over North American and British leaders nor by determining its role in shaping the theological statements of international conferences, but by noting the extent to which it is forming the life and mission of local evangelical churches around the world.

Luis Tapia Rubio, *PhD student, International Baptist Theological Study Center (IBTS Center), Vrije Universiteit Amsterdam. Luis is a member of College Mennonite Church, Goshen, Indiana; Research Fellow, Institute for the Study of Global Anabaptism (ISGA), Goshen College, Indiana; and lecturer, Hispanic Anabaptist Biblical Seminary (SeBAH), United States.*

Adam McKay, director, *Don't Look Up*, Hyperobject Industries, Bluegrass Films, Netflix, 2021. 138 minutes.
https://www.netflix.com/ca/title/81252357.

Released December 5, 2021, *Don't Look Up* is a star-studded movie written and directed by Adam McKay that quickly became Netflix's #2 most-viewed feature of all-time. It is a powerful reflection on climate change and political inaction—inaction that, according to McKay and friends, is rooted fundamentally in science denial, in addition to greed and desire for technological fixes. For some, this crisis of science denial makes the movie not simply an allegory for climate change but also a commentary on the COVID-19 pandemic, helping us understand some of the public responses to vaccinations and safety mandates.

Don't Look Up is a dark comedy that offers a profound critique of current political and corporate realities and how they block concerted action on climate, particularly in the United States. It is also an effort to engage us—the viewing public—and to stir and animate us to action. To that end, I'd like to use this movie review to explore my response to climate change and to challenge you to do the same. In the process, I will try not to give away anything in the movie in case you have not seen it. I do recommend watching it and gathering with others for a time of reflection, discussion, and even prayer. *Don't Look Up* offers many gems of insight. For me, it is like a parable.

> "We have exactly 6 months, 10 days, 2 hours, 11 minutes, and 41 seconds until a comet twice the size of Chicxulub tears through our atmosphere and extincts all life on Earth."
>
> —Kate Dibiasky, scientist who discovers Comet NEOWISE, in *Don't Look Up*

The film begins with the discovery of a comet on a collision course with Earth. In six months, all life will be wiped out unless drastic action is taken. Much of the movie is about the efforts of two "ordinary" North American scientists who try to get their government and the world to take the discovery seriously.

Today, despite ever-increasing extreme weather events, despite ever-more conclusive scientific reports (we think of the Intergovernmental Panel on Climate Change Sixth Assessment Report[18]), it is clear that the critical issue of climate change is ignored by many. For various reasons,[19] so many people "don't look and don't think" and "do ignore and do deny." And yet our fate with climate change—even if we fail to do anything—is not nearly as clear or as sudden

18 The Intergovernmental Panel on Climate Change, "Sixth Assessment Report," 2021–22, accessed March 4, 2022, https://www.ipcc.ch/assessment-report/ar6/.

19 See George Marshall, *Don't Even Think about It: Why Our Brains Are Wired to Ignore Climate Change* (New York: Bloomsbury, 2015).

as having a comet slam into us (in the same way that an asteroid devastated Earth some 66 million years ago).

We can act and make a difference with climate change in ways that we can't with a comet. The choices and actions we make—not just those made by the politicians or the big tech and military forces as described in the movie—really do matter. Though there is some political engagement by the public in the movie, it is underplayed. And, of course, the question of lifestyle changes and communal activism (eating differently, consuming less, farming and heating buildings more sustainably, and so on) doesn't really apply to comets. But let's set that aside, and focus on what we can take away from the movie. And I'd like us to do so by engaging a thought experiment.

I invite you to imagine what would happen if you and I received this news today: "You have six months to live, unless we can work a miracle!" Let us assume you process this harsh news from a Christian perspective. I suppose this might be like receiving the shock news from a doctor that I have stage IV lung cancer or something like that. Except in this situation, we all get the same news—*six months*.

How would you respond? How would I?

I imagine I'd deny it at first. Or seriously hope the news is wrong. What would convince me otherwise? Would more evidence? Second opinions and a battery of medical tests? Or is it when I share this with friends and family and I hear back stories like, "Yes, I had a friend who died in six months, just like the doctors said." Or maybe: "I know a gal who tried this and was totally cured." Or how about: "The tests can give false positives. Have faith!" Sound familiar? *Is it the science or the relationships that carry the day with us?*

The next stage is anger. I want to blame someone. If the news was cancer, I might try blaming the government, industry, or anyone with deep pockets as I argue for compensation. Regarding COVID-19, who can I blame? And who do they blame? Technology? Our economic system? The pharmaceutical industry who profits big-time (or maybe not as much as we think)? Corrupt politicians who are in the pockets of big business? But what or who can I blame regarding an impending disaster from a comet? God is sovereign, I believe. So do I pray for more time? For God to divert the comet? Have mercy, Lord. I want to live! Why is this happening?

Some might argue that maybe I should even pray for the end to come sooner. After all, I can't wait to be with Jesus, right? Paul said, "I desire to depart and be with Christ, which is better by far" (Phil 1:23). I have to confess that this seems to be more theory to me than trusted fact. Something I take by faith, but I am *of little faith* (Matt 14:31).

Questions abound in this liminal time, this crisis time, about my relationship with my maker. I wonder if I have found the *narrow gate* (Matt 7:13–14)? Do I *have love for others as Jesus loved me* (John 13:34)? Can people actually love like that? I fall short for sure. Have I been *feeding, clothing, and comforting* Jesus (his image-bearers described in Matt 25:35–36)? Have I been *losing my life for Jesus's sake* (Matt 10:39), or have I been seeking to find out who I am? Will Jesus say to me, *"Well done, good and faithful servant"* (Matt 25:21), or will he tell me, *"I never knew you"* (Matt 7:23)? Yes, I know it is *by grace I have been saved through faith* (Eph 2:8), but am I *doing the good works which God prepared in advance for me to do* (Eph 2:10)?

I wonder how I would spend the last six months of my life? How would you? Perhaps *relax, eat, drink, be merry* (Luke 12:19)? Would *go and make disciples of all nations* (Matt 28:19) take on new meaning and urgency for me? Would I look for opportunities to be like the Good Samaritan (Luke 10:25–37)? Would I, as a middle-class Canadian (and by definition a rich man), wake up to the misery of the world's poor—the Lazarus's of the world that *lie at my gate* (Luke 16:19–22)? They suffer disproportionately and unjustly from the climate change I and the wealthy nations of this world cause. Even worse, the poor did almost nothing to contribute to climate change. Would I, in this moment, finally be able to cast mammon aside, and only *worship God* (Matt 6:24)? Surely I would make my priority, at long last, to *first seek his kingdom and his righteousness* (Matt 6:33), wouldn't I? What would you do?

> "I'm sorry. Are we not being clear?"
> "We're trying to tell you that the entire planet is about to be destroyed."
> —Kate Dibiasky

Like the gospels, *Don't Look Up* invites all who have ears to hear, to radical change of heart. And to action. It is a parable, calling us to address a climate crisis that, according to the United Nations Secretary General Antonio Guterres, represents an "existential threat."[20]

For Christians, *Don't Look Up* can serve as an opportunity to examine our lives and our lived responses— yes to climate, yes to creation, and, ultimately, yes to our Creator. Here's an opportunity for reorientation.

> "We really did have everything, didn't we? I mean, when you think about it."
> —Randall Mindy, scientist in *Don't Look Up*

I encourage you to watch the movie and then, on your own and with others, consider: What biblical passages come to your heart as you contemplate the film? How is the Holy Spirit moving and speaking to you and your circle?

> "Dearest Father and Almighty Creator, we ask for Your grace tonight, despite our pride. Your forgiveness, despite our doubt. Most of all Lord we ask for Your Love to soothe us through these dark times. May we face whatever is

---

20 UN News Global Perspective Human Stories, May 15, 2018, United Nations, https://news.un.org/en/story/2018/05/1009782.

> to come in Your divine will with courage, and open hearts of acceptance. Amen."
>
> —Yule, prayer at dinner table scene in *Don't Look Up*

Watching *Don't Look Up*, I felt moved to commit the rest of my career and my life to climate justice. How will you spend the last six months or six years or sixty years of your life? Lord give us grace, love, and courage.

NELSON LEE *attends Chinatown Peace Church in downtown Vancouver—the unceded territories of xʷməθkʷəy̓əm (Musqueam), Sḵwx̱wú7mesh (Squamish), and Sel'íl'witulh (Tsleil-Waututh) Nations. A professional engineer, Nelson founded Green Sky Sustainability, which helps organizations and companies with sustainability solutions.*

Paul Plett, director, *I Am a Mennonite*, Ode Productions, 2021. 58 minutes.

https://itunes.apple.com/ca/movie/i-am-a-mennonite/id1586383037.

"What makes a Mennonite a Mennonite?"

With this question, Canadian filmmaker Paul Plett invites us to follow him on an exploration of his own personal story. Through interviews and monologues, this documentary traces Plett's family heritage while also trying to answer larger questions of what being a Mennonite is all about. His goal is to observe where Mennonites are going spiritually by first answering the questions of where they are and where they have been. Many others have taken on this noble task, but since Plett identifies as a Mennonite himself, he starts with his own background in order to uncover what threads weave him into the larger Mennonite story.

Pulling off his stereotypical straw hat, suspenders, and fake beard, Plett emphasizes that Mennonites come in all shapes, colors, styles, and fashions. Mennonites look as "normal" as he does, or like any person could look. However, it becomes clear through interviews with his family and friends that the definition of "Mennonite" is in the eye of the beholder. For some it is strictly about family bloodline and cultural practices. For others it is about values and principles. And for still others it is about a specific expression of the Christian faith.

To find out more about what being a Mennonite means, Plett traces his family's footsteps to the former Molotschna Colony in present-day Ukraine. He tries to find remnants of his family's presence prior to their migration to Canada. The only evidence of their village, however, is old tombstones and the stories that come with them. Plett continues on to Amsterdam in the Netherlands to track down information about a relative who is his family's oldest known link to the Mennonite movement of the sixteenth century. Unfortunately, he comes up short once again. It is at this point that he starts to switch his focus.

From Amsterdam, Plett travels north to Friesland in the Netherlands to see the town where Menno Simons (the Mennonites' namesake) got his start in the Anabaptist movement. In conversation with the pastor of the Mennonite church in Simons's hometown, Plett focuses in on the spiritual heritage of the Mennonite faith. He marvels at how one man made such a large impact for those who were questioning the status quo and seeking spiritual renewal.

At this point in his journey, Plett no longer needs evidence of his family's ethnic connection to the early Anabaptists. He is a Mennonite because he can identify directly with Menno Simons through the community Simons founded. In his final monologue, Plett concludes that the most significant part of being a Mennonite is belonging to this global community. As he returns home, he expresses his desire for his family to also find their place within it.

There is something special about accompanying a pilgrim on their journey to self-discovery. It inevitably causes us to reflect on our own identity and belonging. In my case, I realized that I could not see myself in Plett's story. Yes, I too am a Mennonite, but the difference between us is that I have no historical connection to the ethnic and cultural heritage he describes. I am a Mennonite by confession, and although I truly appreciate the cultural values and practices that come from the Swiss/Russian tradition, they have as much to do with being a Mennonite as my Filipino/German/Canadian background does.

Although Plett distinguishes between ethnic, cultural, and religious aspects of Mennonites, he ends up with the same convoluted message with which his interviewees began the documentary—that being a Mennonite can mean all of these things and more. It seems that everyone can pick and choose what defines them as Mennonite, because the most important part is seeing oneself as part of the community. What is most striking is that he makes this conclusion in the very place where Menno Simons first became convicted against such ideas.

If Plett truly wanted to discover where Mennonites have been, he would have focused on what identified this sect of Christians in contrast to those around them. Nowhere in the early Anabaptist confessions do we find any notion that Mennonite identity can be passed down through bloodline or culture. In fact, it was the complete opposite. Mennonites died for the belief that faith in God must be chosen and that the true test of faith is discipleship, not ethnic, cultural, social, or political heritage.

If Plett had truly wanted to discover where Mennonites currently are going spiritually, he would have at some point ended up in dialogue with the faith community of Mennonite World Conference. The more we can avoid holding up one tradition as being "truly Mennonite," the more we will celebrate the global diversity among us and the cultural differences that make us who we are. Although we owe a lot to our early European siblings, what ultimately draws us together is not their story but our common story of faith in Jesus and our desire to work together in God's church.

Yes, heritage and history are important. Yes, we can learn a lot from the people who came before us. However, there is a danger in our North American insistence that being Mennonite is rooted in ethnicity and cultural heritage. If this is our belief, then our witness may look more like cultural assimilation than introducing people of all backgrounds to Jesus and the Mennonite lens through which our faith can be lived out.

The issue with this film is not that Plett sought out his familial roots or that his conclusion focused on community, but that in his open definition of community, being Mennonite actually means very little. This might be satisfactory for someone whose heritage prescribed a Mennonite identity, but for anyone who has chosen to join the Mennonite tradition, this conclusion comes up short.

One marker of a successful documentary is whether it answers its own questions. Plett began by asking where Mennonites are heading spiritually. Unfortunately, because of the trajectory of his journey, we never get a clear answer. If we really want to know where Mennonites are heading, we would do well to gather together people of various backgrounds who are choosing this faith tradition and ask them, "What makes you a Mennonite?"

Moses Falco *lives in Treaty 1 territory with his family. He pastors at Sterling Mennonite Fellowship in Winnipeg, Manitoba, blogs regularly at MosesFalco.com, and co-hosts a podcast at TheMennoCast.com.*

www.ingramcontent.com/pod-product-compliance
Lightning Source LLC
LaVergne TN
LVHW041103150826
845673LV00007B/1908

9798830673747